Capital Adequacy Requirements and Bank Holding Companies

Research for Business Decisions, No. 32

Gunter Dufey, Series Editor
Professor of International Business and Finance
The University of Michigan

Other Titles in This Series

No. 25 *Disinvestment of Foreign Subsidiaries*   Brent D. Wilson

No. 26 *Foreign Exchange Management in Multinational Firms*   Vinh Quang Tran

No. 27 *Data Communications and the Systems Designer*   Francis Gerald Smith

No. 28 *Determinants of Large Bank Dividend Policy*   William F. Kennedy

No. 29 *Are There GA(A)PS in Financial Reporting for The Life Insurance Industry?*   Robert B. Yahr

No. 30 *The Corporate Investor Relations Function: A Survey*   Mollie Haley Wilson

No. 31 *Pooled Data for Financial Markets*   Terry E. Dielman

Capital Adequacy Requirements and Bank Holding Companies

by
Itzhak Swary

RESEARCH PRESS

Text first published as a
typescript facsimile in 1978

Produced and distributed by
UMI Research Press
an imprint of
University Microfilms International
Ann Arbor, Michigan 48106

Library of Congress Cataloging in Publication Data

Swary, Itzhak, 1946-
    Capital adequacy requirements and bank holding
companies.

    (Research for business decisions ; no. 32)
    Bibliography: p.
    Includes index.
    1. Bank holding companies—United States.   I. Title.
II. Series.
HG2567.S9 1980   332.1'6   80-22439
ISBN 0-8357-1129-3

Contents

Tables   vii

Figures   ix

Acknowledgments   xi

Chapter I.
Introduction
    I.1   The Nature of the Problem   1
    I.2   Previous Research Relating to Capital Adequacy   3
    I.3   Objectives of the Study   7

Chapter II.
The Decision-Making Process of Unregulated Banks   9
    II.1   The Framework of the Analysis   9
    II.2   The Investment Decision—Credit Portfolio Selection   13
    II.3   The Bank Financing Decision and Liquidity Management   21
    II.4   A Theory of a Bank's Decision-Making Process   30

Chapter III.
An Analysis of the Banking Industry
Under Capital Adequacy Regulation   37
    III.1 Capital Adequacy Regulations   37
    III.2 The Decision-Making Process of Banks Under
           Capital Adequacy Regulations   43
    III.3 Social and Private Costs of the Regulatory Process   52
    III.4 Improving the Regulatory Process   57

Chapter IV.
The Development and Regulation of Bank Holding Companies   61
    IV.1   Background and Historical Perspective   61
    IV.2   The Rationale for Nonbank Expansion of BHCs   64
    IV.3   Capital Adequacy and the Regulation of BHCs   66
    IV.4   Cost-Benefit Considerations of BHC Expansion
           into Nonbank Activities   69

Chapter V.
Bank Holding Companies' Acquisition of Nonbank Firms,
the Federal Reserve Board's Decision Orders
and Stockholder Returns: Empirical Analysis   73
    V.1   Alternative Hypotheses of BHCs' Acquisitions
        of Nonbank Activities   73
    V.2   Alternative Hypotheses of the Board's Denial Orders
        of BHC Applications for Expansion
        into Nonbank Activities   75
    V.3   Methodology and Estimation Procedures,
        Data Sources and Sample Selection   77
    V.4   Empirical Results   84
    V.5   Interpretation of the Results   102
    V.6   An Evaluation of Current Regulation of BHCs   105

Chapter VI.
Summary and Implications for the Regulation of
Bank Holding Companies   111

Appendix 2A
Exposition of the Credit Portfolio Selection Model   117

Appendix 2B
The Individual Bank's Decision-Making Process   119

Appendix 3A
The Comparative Statics Analysis of the Direct Chance Constraint 123

Appendix 5A
Probability Tests of CAR   127

Appendix 5B
The Performance of the Mortgage Banking Industry   129

Notes   135

Bibliography   145

Index   149

Tables

4-1   Activities Permitted as "Closely Related to Banking" as of December 10, 1977   63

5-1   Proposed Acquisitions of Nonbank Firms by BHCs Processed by the Board, January 1, 1971 to September 10, 1977   78

5-2   Non-Mortgage Applications: Percentage Weekly Average Residuals (AR), Cumulative Average Residuals (CAR) and Sample Size (N_w) for All (49) Applications and Two Subgroups, Denied (14) and Approved (35)   86

5-3   Probability Tests on the Residuals of BHCs that Applied to Acquire Non-Mortgage Companies   88

5-4   Mortgage Applications: Percentage Weekly Average Residuals (AR), Cumulative Average Residuals (CAR) and Sample Size (N_w) for All Applications (25) and Two Subgroups, Denied (7) and Approved (18)   90

5-5   Probability Tests on the Residuals of BHCs that Applied to Acquire Mortgage Companies   92

5-6   Sample Statistics of Risk Measures   98

5-7   Frequency of Changes in the Variance-Risk $VAR(\tilde{R}_j)$ of Weekly Returns for All BHCs   99

5-8   Joint Frequency of Changes in Risk Measures   101

5-9   Estimates of Risk Shifts in Portfolios of Bank Stocks   109

Tables

5B-1   Mortgage Industry: Percentage Weekly Average
        Residuals (AR) and Cumulative Average Residuals
        (CAR) for Portfolios Corresponding to
        All (25) Mortgage Applications and Two Subgroups,
        Denied (7) and Approved (18)   132

5B-2   Probability Tests on the Residuals of Mortgage
        Industry Portfolios   134

Figures

2-1   The Safety-First Constraint   17

2-2   The Investment Decision   32

2-3   The Effect of Financial Structure on Investment Opportunities   33

2-4   The Decision-Making Process   35

5-1   Non-Mortgage Applications: Cumulative Average Residuals for 16 Weeks Surrounding the Announcement Week (AW) and the Decision Week (DW)   93

5-2   Mortgage Applications: Cumulative Average Residuals for 16 Weeks Surrounding the Announcement Week (AW) and the Decision Week (DW)   94

5B-1   Mortgage Industry Portfolio Corresponding to Mortgage Applications: Cumulative Average Residuals for 16 Weeks Surrounding the Announcement Week (AW) and the Decision Week (DW)   131

Acknowledgments

I should like to thank my dissertation committee—Professor George Benston (Chairman), Professor Kenneth Gaver, and Professor Leonard Simon—for their excellent guidance during the course of this study.

I am especially indebted to my advisor, Professor George Benston. Very generous with his time, Professor Benston has been a continual source of intellectual stimulation and encouragement. He closely supervised this study, read several drafts in a careful and critical manner, and offered many useful suggestions. For all his efforts on my behalf, both professional and personal, I shall always be grateful.

I should like also to thank Professor Kenneth Gaver, a teacher and a friend, for his encouragement and advice. He willingly shared with me his reknowned knowledge in the fields of computers and econometrics.

I am also indebted to Professor Leonard Simon for an encouragement that went beyond his professional obligations. His generous availability, his insightful suggestions, and his many useful comments contributed to the improvement of this study.

I am also grateful to: Joseph Aharony, John Long, Yoram Peles, Ramon Rabinovitch, Clifford Smith, and Lee Wakeman, for their helpful suggestions and thoughtful criticisms.

The special dissertation grant provided by the Bank Administration Institute is also greatly appreciated.

Finally, I would like to thank my parents, Jhuda and Naima, my brother, Matslicha, and my sisters, Thila and Avigail, for their personal support and for their patient and constant encouragement.

Chapter I

Introduction

I.I   The Nature of the Problem

The question of capital adequacy has attracted long and continuous attention from bank management and from regulatory authorities.[1] Nevertheless, despite substantial public discussion, little progress appears to have been made in assessing capital adequacy systematically and in evaluating the consequences of capital adequacy regulations. The American Bankers Association (1954) stated:

> There has been a good deal of confusion with respect to the adequacy of bank capital funds. Interest in the subject has increased greatly in recent years as a result of the growth of deposits, the change in the composition of assets, the state of bank earnings, and fluctuations in the market value of bank investments. There has been a lack of agreement on the part of both supervisory authorities and bankers themselves as to how to determine whether a bank's capital funds are sufficient. (P. 1)

The objective of this study is to analyze the impact of current capital adequacy regulations on the banking industry within a suggested framework of unregulated bank's decision-making processes. Based on this analysis, the effects of a recent legislation on the banking industry—the 1970 Amendment to the Bank Holding Company Act—will be examined and tested.

The magnitude of the costs associated with bank failures is a basic factor in determining the importance of the capital adequacy question. A firm's (bank's) failure is defined to occur if the firm is unable to meet its obligations. The larger the bank's capital-to-debt ratio, the smaller the probability of its not meeting its obligations. Accordingly, equity capital serves as a source of funds with the specific feature of determining (*cet. par.*) the states in which the firm is insolvent, and hence the expected costs of bankruptcy. In the banking industry, bankruptcy costs take on a specific form (discussed later). These costs are assumed to be large enough to affect considerably the market value maximization process of unregulated banks.

Bank failures also concern the regulatory authorities. Explanations of bank regulation have been considered in several studies (Meltzer, 1967; Benston, 1973; Black, Miller, Posner, 1978). These studies suggest that the explanations that have sound theoretical and empirical bases are: (1) the protection of bank customers who operate with a high degree of ignorance about bank risk, so that it is more efficient for the government than for individual depositors to examine banks; and (2) the prevention of external diseconomies generated by the loss of public confidence due to bank failure. In the United States, deposit insurance provided by the Federal Deposit Insurance Corporation (FDIC) eliminates the danger of losses for most depositors, as well as greatly reduces the probability of bank runs; thus, supervision and capital requirements are ways of protecting the FDIC's funds. These rationales for capital adequacy requirements in banking are consistent with the "public interest" theory of regulation, whereby regulation is a device taken to protect consumers (public interest).[2]

The economic theories of capital adequacy intervention become much more complicated processes if politicians and regulators themselves are considered interest groups that seek to maximize their welfare. Thus, regulators are imperfect agents who derive utility directly through the content of their decisions, and indirectly through the effects of their decisions upon their salaries and tenure (this issue is discussed further in Chapter III). This study takes the naive approach that regulation is exogenously applied to the industry and that regulators behave according to what they claim they are doing. The interesting question as to why they behave the way they do is not considered.

The actual policies and practices used by regulatory agencies in the United States vary widely, despite the fact that their underlying objectives and attitudes toward bank capital are basically the same. Vojta (1973, pp. 11-15) reports that the Federal Reserve Board's standards quantify the level of capital necessary to protect against dilution of the quality of assets. This is achieved by assigning different capital requirements to each class of assets according to its perceived risk. On the liabilities side, volatility ratios are applied to derive the total gross capital required for liquidity purposes. The required capital is computed as the sum of the capital provisions for fixed assets, asset protection and liquidity. The total-capital-requirement calculation is compared with both the adjusted capital structure of the bank (defined to be the total capital accounts minus assets classified as a loss and 50 percent of assets classified as doubtful), and the adjusted equity (adjusted capital structure minus debt capital).[3] The Federal Deposit Insurance Corporation (FDIC) relies on a ratio of capital funds, net of fixed and substandard assets, to total assets. The Comptroller of the Currency emphasizes reliance on guidelines for appraising the capital position of a bank in relation to the quality of its management, and the bank's asset and deposit position as a going concern under normal conditions (with provision for a margin of safety).[4]

Numerous studies have been devoted to the analysis of different aspects of capital adequacy regulation, such as evaluation of the proper extent of regulatory intervention, determination of the social cost of overcapitalization, and the examination of the effectiveness and efficiency of current capital adequacy regulations and suggestions for improving them. Several of the most recent works in this area are summarized and discussed next.[5]

1.2 Previous Research Relating to Capital Adequacy

A. Optimal vs. Adequate Capital

Optimal bank capital is determined by the decision-making process of the bank, which is presumably governed by an objective of maximizing some appropriate criterion such as stockholder wealth. Capital adequacy is determined by that probability of bank failure which is viewed as socially optimal by regulators. The main concern of most analyses of capital adequacy is to determine to what extent optimal and adequate capital differ.

Robinson and Pettway (1967), Pringle (1974), and Taggart and Greenbaum (1978) are concerned with the role of capital in the financial management of the individual bank. They conclude that the amount of equity capital is an important managerial decision variable and that maximizing behavior with respect to shareholders' wealth does not necessarily lead to a low capital position. They reason that banks are pressured by profit-maximizing behavior to hold the optimal leverage position dictated by the capital market forces. Thus, they call for the abandonment of regulatory standards on capital in favor of the market's discipline. Specifically, Pringle (1974) assumes that the bank is a private wealth-maximizing economic unit that operates in imperfect markets, and concludes that the optimal capital policy is determined by the relative transaction costs of alternative financing sources and investment opportunities. Taggart and Greenbaum (1978) base their analysis on the assumption that transaction services (to depositors) provide the bank with profit opportunities that are offset by regulatory constraints (e.g., reserve requirements) and lead to an optimal amount of deposits and financial structure. It should be emphasized that the impact of equity capital on the probability of a bank's failure and the expected costs of bankruptcy, which are the main interest of regulators, are entirely ignored in these studies. In contrast to the approaches of the foregoing studies, the explanation advanced by authorities and other economists (see Watson, 1974) to justify supervision of the banking system is the possible difference between each bank's optimal capital structure (reflecting private benefits and costs) and what society considers an adequate amount of capital (reflecting social benefits and costs).

B. The Impact of Regulation on Bank's Capital

Several studies attempt to evaluate the effectiveness of the regulatory agencies in the United States. Mayne (1972) analyzes the differences in the amount of capital required by each of the regulatory agencies, i.e., whether different regulatory agencies have different impacts on bank capital. Since there are marked differences in the capital standards required by each agency (as discussed above), effective implementation of the various regulatory standards could lead to significant differences in observed capital positions among banks. In her empirical study, Mayne reports that such differences are statistically insignificant. This empirical evidence is compatible with either of the following hypotheses: 1) there are similarities in *applied* capital standards of the supervisory agencies, or 2) regulators are not able to impose their capital standards upon the banks they presumably regulate.

Peltzman (1970) computed estimates of the magnitude of the effect of government regulation on capital investment in commercial banking, and also examined whether deposit insurance is a substitute for capital. His results indicate that during the period studied "there was no evidence that bank investment behavior conforms to the standard set forth for it by the regulatory agencies" (p. 20). The basis for this conclusion is a significantly negative (cross-sectional) relationship over a three-year period between the flow of capital into banking and various measures that approximate regulatory determined capital adequacy. Furthermore, the deposit insurance variable (percentage of insured deposits) was found to be negatively related to capital investment. He concludes, therefore, that deposit insurance is substituted for capital and that capital requirements of regulators are ineffective, i.e., the capital investment process in banks is not affected in any important way by regulation.

Peltzman's study, however, was criticized by Mingo (1975). Mingo's study follows Peltzman's approach closely and attempts to correct two apparent errors: (1) a specification error in measuring the impact of the regulatory process; the relationship between capital and regulatory pressure is nonlinear, i.e., the regulator puts much more pressure on banks that are considered very deficient in capital; (2) use of data unsuitable for such an inquiry, namely, data aggregated by states. The main finding of Mingo's study is that the lower the ratio of actual capital to capital required by the regulators, the more likely is the bank to increase its capital over the next period in order to satisfy the demand of the bank regulator.

The effectiveness of capital requirements imposed by regulators leads to the fundamental questions raised in this controversy over capital adequacy, i.e., is regulatory supervision of capital standards appropriate, and is the current bank regulation process efficient?

C. Social Costs and Benefits of Capital Adequacy Regulation

Santomero and Watson (1977) discuss the determinants of the social costs and benefits of increased capitalization in a general equilibrium framework. The benefits result from the decrease in the expected costs of bank failure both to society as a whole and to the individual bank. The social costs are the opportunity costs of overcapitalization that must be borne both by the banking system and by society at large. Any excess capital in banking has undesirable effects on the output and productivity in the economy through misallocation of resources. However, the impact (social and private costs) of the regulatory process on both the individual bank market value maximization (in particular, the bank's investment policy) and the volume of intermediation in the economy is ignored in the Santomero and Watson study.

The impact of capital adequacy regulation on the behavior of individual banks is analyzed, to some extent, by Blair and Heggestad (1978) and Kahane (1977) indicates that regulators often use capital requirements of portfolio regulations in order to maintain a sound banking system (i.e., one with a lower probability of bank failures). These requirements, however, cannot completely ensure a decrease in the probability of ruin since they may affect adversely other decisions (and their attendant risks) as well. Blair and Heggestad (1978) suggest that portfolio regulations are rather inefficient and might also be ineffective since regulators' attempts to maintain soundness can be achieved without altering the mean-variance efficient frontier faced by the bank by constraining the feasible set of assets a bank can hold. A serious shortcoming of both studies is the use of improper objective functions (mean-variance utility functions) for the individual banks which makes it unlikely that they have derived actual consequences of the regulatory process on the individual bank's behavior and on the social costs involved.

The social benefits of capital adequacy regulation result from the decrease in the expected costs of bank failure. The theoretical relationship between failure and capital is clear. In practice, however, this link depends on the ability of examiners to identify problem banks before failure, i.e., the efficiency of the identification process. This issue is analyzed and tested in several empirical studies. Cotter (1966) tests the usefulness of the capital ratio in predicting bank failures. He finds that the mean values of capital ratios for those banks that failed and those that did not are not statistically different. Benston (1973) compares the ratio of capital to assets adjusted by the quality (riskiness) of the bank's assets according to the FDIC evaluation at approximately a year before failure. His findings indicate that ". . . a relatively large number of banks that failed were severely undercapitalized. . ." (p. 45). Inadequate capital, however, does not occupy a prominent position on the list of causes of failure provided by Benston, a fact which, in his study at least, implies that capital plays a small role in the prevention of failure. Sinky (1978) examines the FDIC's adjusted capital ratio and finds that loan classification is an important variable in identifying problem banks. He finds that almost all banks that failed in recent years, evidently had a large volume of substandard loans for several years

preceding their failure. The FDIC identification process was found to be inefficient, however, since almost all banks with low adjusted capital ratios did not
fail. Santomero and Vinso (1977) also estimate the cross-section riskiness of the
banking structure and its sensitivity to variations in bank capital. Their results
indicate that: ". . . the industry is exposed, on average, to a very small risk of
suspended operations, and this probability changes very little with variations in
the capital account buffer. However, some banks within the sample do exhibit
higher risk potential. These can be explained, to a large part, by relatively low
capital ratios and/or high variability over the sample period" (p. 204).

The Sinky and Santomero-Vinso studies imply that the existence of
inadequate capital or high probability of bankruptcy is not a common characteristic of the industry as a whole but rather is specific to a group of problem
banks. The implied conclusion, therefore, is that, rather than being imposed
upon the entire industry, these capital adequacy constraints should be limited to
these banks.

In summary, findings on the social benefits of capital adequacy regulation
raise many questions on regulatory practice. Furthermore, Kreps and Wacht
(1971) argue that with the existence of deposit insurance there is no public
interest rationale for supervisory standards of minimum capital adequacy in
banks. This point is further discussed in Chapter III. Finally, the fact that
capital deficiency is specific to only a small group of problem banks emphasizes
the importance of the identification of these banks in the regulatory process.[6]

D. Improving the Regulatory Process

Improvements in the identification process used by regulators to classify banks
that are likely to fail (problem banks) and alternative approaches to capital
adequacy regulation are suggested in several works. Cohen (1970) proposes
several modifications in the Federal Reserve examiners' version of the capital
adequacy formula in order to measure properly a bank's risk position. These
modifications involve considerations of changes that have occurred in the
securities (bond) markets and in the nature of the liquidity risk. Cotter (1966)
finds a significant difference in the relative levels of excess capital ratios in
banks that have survived financial depression compared to those that have not.
(Excess capital is defined as total capital less stock capital.) The rationale for
using this measure of capital remains unclear, and its use, therefore, for
predicting bank failures is questionable. Meyer and Pifer (1970) suggest an
alternative model to those used by the regulatory agencies by which to identify
banks that are potential failures. They use a regression function that constrains
the dependent variable to two values (0, 1) (i.e., a dummy dependent variable),
and are able to predict bank failures with a two-period lead using readily
available balance-sheet and income statement data. Most of their results,

however, are statistically insignificant, and further, their predictive power has not been compared to that of current standards used by the regulatory agencies in order to test their relative efficiency. Santomero and Vinso (1977) use discriminant analysis to determine whether the distributions of the variables used to estimate the probability of a bank's failure differ significantly for risky banks when compared to the other population subset. Their results indicate that "a simple two-dimensional Z screen may be used as a device to spot-light potentially troubled banks" (p. 203). Within the screen, the traditional capital asset ratio used by regulators proves to be quite important. Vojta (1973) argues that the Federal Reserve Board's standard leads to overcapitalization since it is based on "simultaneous worse case loss experience in all categories of risk" (p. 15). Instead, he proposes tests that quantify historical loss experiences within any given institution in terms of the different types of risk, and utilization of this information to forecast expected losses. Two specific capital adequacy tests are proposed by Vojta: 1) an "earnings test," which requires that current earnings amount to at least twice the level of total expected normal annual loss; and 2) a "capital cushion test," which requires a bank to hold an amount of capital funds 20 times the last 5 years' moving average of actual total loss experience. Although the criticism raised by Vojta is correct, the proposed tests for determining whether a bank is sound are, to a large extent, "rules of thumb." The most important advantage of Vojta's approach is the simultaneous measurements of overall risk exposure and derived capital adequacy in commercial banks. The reliance on past experience and, in particular, evaluation of past experience in terms of required capital, however, is subjective and clearly is not applicable to all banks equally.

In conclusion, the current state of the banking literature leaves unanswered many issues concerning capital adequacy regulation. One important issue is the impact of the various existing capital adequacy regulations on the behavior of the individual bank. Analysis of such impact is required to determine the private and social costs of the regulatory process and to select efficient measures to enable regulators to monitor a bank's probability of failure. Finally, an appropriate measure of the social costs of the regulatory process is needed to evaluate the rationale of government intervention.

I.3   Objectives of the Study

The major purpose of this study is to examine the impact of the various types of capital adequacy regulation on the decision-making process of the individual bank and on the social costs of the regulatory process. The analysis should provide a basis for evaluating the efficiency and effectiveness of current and proposed regulatory schemes. Efficiency is measured in terms of the private and social costs and benefits that result from the regulatory process. The effectiveness of capital adequacy regulation is determined by its impact on the overall risk, i.e., the probability of bank failures, in the banking system.

An appropriate framework for evaluating capital adequacy regulation includes a theory of the decision-making process of unregulated banks and a theory of the regulatory process. It is hoped that the discussion of the behavior of unregulated banks will lead to a better understanding of their economic role, and that discussion of the regulatory process will yield insights into the rationale of bank regulation and the purposes of different types of capital adequacy regulation. An important research area delineated from the discussion is the analysis and testing of the rationale for the growing role in recent years of the bank holding company form of organization and its implications for capital adequacy regulation.

The plan of this study is as follows. In Chapter II the decision-making process of unregulated banks is analyzed. Investment and financing decisions are first treated separately, and then combined in order to provide a theory of an individual bank's decision making. Chapter III examines the various types of capital adequacy regulations used in different countries, and then discusses the decision-making process of regulated banks and the effectiveness and efficiency of the current regulatory process. Finally, recommendations for improvement in the existing regulatory system are proposed. Chapter IV analyzes the impact of the 1970 Amendments to the Bank Holding Company Act on the banking industry and its implications for the current regulatory process, particularly capital adequacy regulations. Chapter V tests the impact on individual banks' market value and riskiness of nonbank activities acquisitions derived from the Bank Holding Company Act. Chapter VI summarizes the study and examines its implications.

Chapter II

The Decision-Making Process
of Unregulated Banks

This chapter provides a description and analysis of the decision-making process of commercial banks. Bank investment and financing decisions are analyzed and emphasis is placed on the way the banks handle uncertainty and the costs of information. It is argued that information costs and the existence of considerable costs associated with bank failure play an important role in the bank decision-making process. The investment decision (credit portfolio selection) is analyzed in section II.2, and the financing decision (the composition of issued claims) is analyzed in section II.3. Finally, these decisions are combined in section II.4 to provide a unified model of the decision-making process of commercial banks.

Benston and Smith (1976) suggest that the economic role of banks is to produce financial assets at lower transaction costs than other segments in the economy. The essence of the analysis in this chapter is that information is a major factor in the production function of banking services, and banks have comparative advantages in the acquisition and analysis of this information. Accordingly, uncertainty and information about their customers' financial conditions play central roles in the various decision-making processes of banks. Moreover, as shown later in Chapter III, similar uncertainty and information costs provide, to some extent, a rationale for the regulatory process.

II.1 The Framework of the Analysis

This section describes the basic framework upon which the analysis in this chapter is based. Included are the balance sheet, the objective function, and the decision variables.

A. The Balance Sheet

There are three types of liabilities of commercial banks: deposits, D_m, where $m = 1, \ldots, M$, which appear on the balance sheet as

$$\sum_{m=1}^{M} D_m$$

funds borrowed from the money market, $F(F>0)$, and equity capital, C. Deposits are heterogeneous, short term, exogenously determined, and stochastic. Borrowed funds are a single homogeneous class of claims and are short-term interest bearing. Capital is an equity security completely controllable by the bank, with infinite maturity (no dividends).

Commercial banks can hold two types of assets: a portfolio of loans, L_i, where $i = 1, \ldots, N$, which appears in the balance sheet as

$$\sum_{i=1}^{N} L_i$$

and invested funds, F ($F<0$). Loans are a heterogeneous class of claims issued by private economic units. Loans vary with respect to their riskiness and uncertainty (information) concerning the activities of the economic agent receiving the loan. Credit selection is assumed to be completely controllable by the bank. Invested funds are assumed to be a single homogeneous class of assets of short maturity, traded in the money market. The demand for invested funds by the bank is assumed to be completely elastic. It is further assumed that banks will never hold invested and borrowed funds simultaneously.

The balance sheet identity is then

$$C+F+ \sum_{m=1}^{M} D_m = \sum_{i=1}^{N} L_i \text{ , where } F \gtrless 0.$$

The bank is assumed to control capital, borrowed (invested) funds, and the credit portfolio decision. The view of the bank's balance sheet taken in this analysis is highly simplified and aggregative. In particular, the liquidity management is simplified and ignores the maturity differential among loans and money market borrowing, and the roles of government securities (bonds), cash and fixed assets.

B. The Objective Function

On the microeconomic level, commercial banks are private firms (economic units). Therefore, they should be analyzed with the same tools that have been employed to analyze firms' behavior in other industries. Because of conceptual difficulties in defining a bank's input and output, this implementation rarely has been used to explain a bank's behavior.[1] In the present study it is assumed that the objective of a commercial bank is to maximize its market value according to the equilibrium valuation function. It is further assumed that the relevant concept of the bank's output is reduction of various transaction costs borne by consumers. This approach is similar to that of Benston and Smith (1976).

The valuation function, which is derived from the Capital Asset Pricing Model (CAPM), has the important basic property of a "linear" relationship between the returns on any two financial assets. (Ross, 1978, shows that the arbitrage consideration under any competitive market leads to this property.) In essence, the linearity property implies that, given any two return streams (investments), the market value of the combined stream is equal to the sum of the separated streams. As Long (1974) points out, however, the usefulness of this model (and the related option-pricing model) depends on the nonexistence of bankruptcy costs. In general, the linearity property for any competitive market where there are no arbitrage opportunities does not hold when bankruptcy costs exist.

Bankruptcy costs were formally introduced by Kraus and Litzenberger (1973), Lloyd-Davies (1975) and Scott (1976). These authors argue that the total value of the firm is reduced by the present value of expected bankruptcy costs. Bankruptcy costs can be classified into two categories: "direct" and "indirect." Direct costs result from the transfer of ownership, namely from reorganization (informally or formally, by the courts). Indirect costs stem from the disruption in production and supplier-customer relationships and include lost sales and profits. The bankruptcy and the ensuing transfer of ownership also convey some information to the firm's potential customers and hence, may affect the market value of the firm in a world of imperfect information. The only empirical study of bankruptcy costs in larger corporations is by Warner (1977). This study of 11 railroad firms seems to support the argument that direct bankruptcy costs are insignificant. He also notes that bankruptcy costs are not likely to be the same across industries. Nevertheless, it is the indirect costs that are likely to be significant, particularly for banks. As Baxter (1967) noted:

> Perhaps the most important cost of bankruptcy proceedings is the negative effect that financial embarrassment may have on the stream of net operating earnings of the business firm. The firm may find it very difficult to obtain trade credit, customers may question its reliability and permanence as a source of supply and may choose to deal elsewhere. Questionable financial condition may be equivalent to negative publicity about the integrity of the firm. Such will certainly be the case for *a bank or other financial institution* but may hold to a lesser extent for the industrial companies. (P. 399, italics added)

In particular, *indirect* costs of bankruptcy are likely to be of paramount importance in the banking industry for the following reasons:

1. Given the existence of restrictions on entry to the industry, the charter of a bank has a market value. Should a bank fail, the market value of its charter will be reduced because of direct regulation intervention in acquisitions and mergers.[2] Moreover the authorities' intervention in acquisitions and mergers reduces the expected value of a tax refund through "carryover" in the case of bankruptcy (see Swary, 1977).

2. Even if entry of firms were not restricted, a bank's investment in goodwill would be substantially lost should it fail.

3. Regulatory authorities are very sensitive to the likelihood of bankruptcy. Therefore, regulators are likely to impose additional constraints (costs) on the bank when the probability of bankruptcy goes beyond a certain level.

In conclusion, it is assumed that a bank's objective is market value maximization. The existence of significant bankruptcy costs in the banking industry significantly affects the valuation of claims on the bank and hence, affects investment decisions taken by the bank. The present study does not explore the nature and properties of capital market equilibrium in a world where bankruptcy costs exist but assumes merely its existence. It should be noted, however, that the use of the CAPM with unequal borrowing and lending rates (as done by Pringle, 1974) is inappropriate in the present context, since the basic properties of the CAPM are violated by the existence of bankruptcy costs.

C. The Decision Variables

The analytic framework that underlies the models in this study is completed by assuming a static one-period decision-making process; i.e., that the behavior of financial intermediaries reflects market value maximization over a single time period. The bank decides on the present optimal amount of loans, borrowing and equity capital. The decision-making process is based on the conditional probability distributions of returns on loans, interest rates in the money market and deposit flows. It is assumed that decisions regarding loans and capital are made at the beginning of the period, and that values remain fixed throughout the period. Changes in money market interest rates and in the flow of deposits take place at the beginning of the planning period, immediately after the values of the decision variables are determined. The deposit flow (inflow-outflow) is matched by money market borrowing and the new balance sheet is determined and remains fixed until the end of the period.

II.2 The Investment Decision—Credit Portfolio Selection

This section analyzes the investment decisions of commercial banks. The discussion includes the characteristics of the loan agreements, the role of uncertainty (and information) in the loans market, and finally, credit portfolio selection.

A. The Loan Agreement

Credit is characterized by three basic elements: i) the amount of credit extended (quantity); ii) the interest rate charged (price); and iii) the quality of the loan (risk). The quality of the loan is determined by the provisions that restrict the borrower's activities, the collateral provided, the available information, and the costs of acquiring additional information concerning a borrower's financial condition.[3]

The need for provisions arises from the lender's wish to prevent acts that would benefit the borrower or other creditors at the expense of the lender because of a conflict of interest. Therefore, a loan contract provision normally requires the borrower to disclose certain events to the lender, contains restrictions on the use of the borrower's assets, and may provide direct supervision of the borrower's business by the lender. It should be observed that if the loan's contract provision allows the borrower to undertake other liabilities or to change the nature of his assets (investments), then the interest rate charged has to be high enough to compensate the lender for expected losses.

Commercial banks' operations in the loan market differ from those of other lenders. For example, in most transactions in the bond market, the financial stream traded and the services attached to the bonds are separate. In practice, however, the borrower and lender frequently agree upon a third party to supply these services, e.g., a trustee. Commercial banks, however, enjoy a comparative advantage in producing these services and, hence, provide both the loan and the associated services. Therefore, in addition to a charge for the risk it bears, the bank charges its customers for the expected costs of services such as processing, writing the loan contract, and monitoring and enforcing its provisions. The interest rate charged, therefore, is determined by the properties of the loan as a contingent claim and by the costs of services related to the loan contract which are provided by the bank.[4]

B. The Role of Uncertainty and Information Costs

It is important to recognize the effect of uncertainty, which makes information a major factor in the production function of the services associated with loans (i.e., searching, writing the contract, monitoring and enforcing costs). Banks enjoy a relative advantage (e.g., compared to the bond market) in acquiring and analyzing information that reduces screening costs and costs of ownership conflicts, i.e., writing a loan contract, collecting and analyzing information about the borrower and enforcing the contract, since additional information often is acquired about customers when the loan is processed and serviced.[5] Thus, the economic role of commercial banks in the loan market is to produce financial commodities (loans) at lower costs than other segments in the economy, *cet. par.*

Commercial banks' comparative advantage in producing loan services through the acquisition and analysis of information is important since it varies with the bank and may provide the bank returns from information (above the cost of acquiring and analyzing it). The broad company-bank business relationships resulting from various services provided by banks (such as corporate demand deposits, letters of credit, employee wages payments, and others) allow the bank almost cost-free and continuous sources of information about corporate activities and performance. In addition, unregulated banks might hold shares of firms with which they are doing business. Any such affiliation between the banks and borrowing firms results in lower information (monitoring) costs. It is reasonable to expect that banks have a real advantage in terms of lending money to these firms since they are closely interrelated.

The returns from information in producing services associated with loans are determined by the competition among banks as well as by the bond market. The level of information costs varies from one bank to another depending on the information available about customers and on the costs of collecting and analyzing additional information. Bank-customer relationships affect a bank's cost (access) of acquiring additional information about customers (as noted by Black, 1975). On the other hand, it is important to recognize that in such a market individual borrowers face a distribution of offer prices across banks and search costs and transaction costs resulting from transferring their business from one bank to another. Therefore, in the case where a corporation receives all or most of its financial services from one bank, the lender has some returns from information.[6] In order to achieve the comparative advantage held by the bank currently supplying financial services to a specific borrower, another bank and the customer must incur additional costs (moving and searching). The returns from information are constrained (bounded) by competition from the bond market and other banks, namely, the amount of information and moving and searching costs. It is also reasonable to assume that the relative advantages per dollar of loan decrease as the amount of loans granted to a single borrower increases. This assumption is based on economies of scale with respect to information cost that other bank competitors enjoy.[7]

Finally, two comments on the nature of loan market equilibrium are of interest. First, because of the added costs resulting from the effect of the loan on the probability of bank failure, banks would not grant loans to corporations unless they had comparative advantages in producing those services associated with loans in order to offset the disadvantages which result from bankruptcy costs. Second, the distribution of loans among banks is also affected by the impact of any given loan on their overall risk (probability of bankruptcy). These considerations are discussed further in a model of credit selection.

C. Credit Portfolio Selection

In this section the determinants of credit allocation by commercial banks are examined. The analysis is based on the lender's objective function and the nature of the corporate loan market as discussed earlier. Assume that a single bank faces N borrowers, each wishing to finance a single corporation (project).[8] Corporation i, ($i = 1, \ldots, N$), requires a constant investment in assets (company size) of A_i, to be financed by a loan of L_i and by the borrower's equity ($E_i = A_i - L_i$). Assume that each project is financed by one bank only.

Assume further that each project yields a random return, $\tilde{R}_i$, that follows a probability distribution function $f_i(\tilde{R}_i)$, which is fully characterized by the first two moments and is independent of the size of external debt.[9] Let $r_i(r_i = 1 + r_i^*)$ be the market-determined interest factor (r_i^* denotes interest rate) paid by borrower i on the loan. Let δ_i be a random variable, such that

$$\delta_i = \begin{cases} 1 \text{ if the borrower fails to repay the loan (defaults)} \\ 0 \text{ otherwise.} \end{cases}$$

Let $P(\delta_i = 1) = P_i$; then $P_i = \int_{-\infty}^{L_i r_i - A_i} f(R_i)d(R_i)$.

If the loan is not collateralized, the bank is assumed to suffer a complete loss if the project fails.[10] Next, the marginal returns from information per dollar of loan granted to borrower i, is denoted by $V_i(L_i)$. These returns reflect the comparative advantages of acquiring and analyzing information enjoyed by the bank in producing services associated with loans. Clearly, V_i is a function of the size of the loan L_i, and it is assumed that $\partial V_i / \partial L_i < 0$. Explicitly, this implies a downward sloping marginal return resulting from the acquisition and analysis of information.[11]

The bank must decide how to allocate a given total amount of dollars, say $\overline{K}$, among N potential loans. In order to concentrate on the investment decision it is assumed that the composition of the financial sources of the bank, such as equity capital, deposits and purchased funds, remain *constant throughout*. The market valuation function used in this model does not directly include the effect of the expected costs of bankruptcy. These expected costs take the form of a safety-first constraint (see Tesler, 1955-56, and Roy, 1952) on the probability of bankruptcy, which is equal to some α, $0 < \alpha < 1$. The α is chosen so that the market value obtained from the analysis is the same as the one that would have been obtained had bankruptcy costs been included. In other words, the constrained α is chosen so that it reduces the bank's market value (compared with no restriction) by the same amount as expected bankruptcy costs. So, if $\tilde{R}_{p1}$ denotes the random amount earned on the bank's capital (C), and R_e is the constant amount paid on external debt (deposits and money market), then:

$$(1) \quad \tilde{R}_{p1} = \sum_{i=1}^{N} L_i[r_i(1 - \delta_i) - 1] - R_e$$

and the safety-first criterion can be written as:

$$(2) \quad P_r(\tilde{R}_{p1} \leqslant -C) = \alpha.$$

Standardizing (2) by μ_{p1} and σ_{p1} (the mean and the standard deviation of the amount earned on the bank's capital, respectively) yields:

$$(3) \quad P_r\left(\frac{\tilde{R}_{p1} - \mu_{p1}}{\sigma_{p1}} \leqslant \frac{-C - \mu_{p1}}{\sigma_{p1}}\right) = \alpha;$$

which can be rewritten as;

$$(4) \quad \mu_{p1} + Z(\alpha)\sigma_{p1} = -C.$$

$Z(\alpha)$ is the inverse of the standard normal cumulative distribution and is a constant, depending on the probability level of α(e.g., $\alpha = 50$ percent $\Rightarrow$ $Z(\alpha) = 0$, $\alpha = 2.5$ percent $\Rightarrow$ $Z(\alpha) = -1.96$, $\alpha = 0.5$ percent $\Rightarrow$ $Z(\alpha) = -2.57$). Clearly,

$$(5) \quad \mu_{p1} = \sum_{i=1}^{N} L_i[r_i(1 - P_i) - 1] - R_e \text{ and}$$

$$(6) \quad \sigma_{p1} = [\sum_{i=1}^{N} \sum_{j=1}^{N} L_i L_j r_i r_j \text{cov}(\delta_i, \delta_j)]^{1/2}.$$

The safety-first constraint is described in Figure 2.1.

Figure 2-1

The Safety-First Constraint

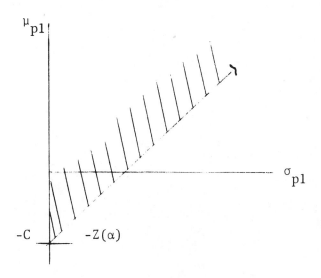

The ray from $-C$ to any portfolio defines a locus of points with equal probability of bankruptcy (α). Where the shaded area to the left and above this ray represents lower (than α) probability of bankruptcy.

Finally, it is assumed that the bank wishes to maximize the increase in its market value $(MV - C)$ subject to its safety-first constraint, given the amount of available funds, $\overline{K}$, and the constraint that loans cannot be negative (i.e., no short sales).

The optimization problem of the bank is to find L_i, $i = 1, \ldots, N$ so as to solve:

(7)   maximize $\{MV - C = \sum\limits_{i=1}^{N} L_i V_i(L_i)\}$

S.t

(7.1) $\sum\limits_{i=1}^{N} L_i = \overline{K}$

(7.2) $L_i \geqslant 0$ $i = 1, \ldots, N$ and

(7.3) $\mu_{p1} + Z(\alpha)\sigma_{p1} = -C$

where μ_{p1} and σ_{p1} are defined by (5) and (6).

The necessary conditions for optimal allocations of loans can be obtained using Kuhn-Tucker conditions.

Let G_1 be defined by:

(8) $G_1 = \sum\limits_{i=1}^{N} L_i V_i(L_i) + \lambda_{11}(\overline{K} - \sum\limits_{i=1}^{N} L_i) +$

$\lambda_{12}(\mu_{p1} + Z(\alpha)\sigma_{p1} + C) + \sum\limits_{i=1}^{N} \gamma_i L_i$

where λ_{11} and λ_{12} are unrestricted and $\gamma_i \geqslant 0$ ($i = 1, \ldots, N$). Then the Kuhn-Tucker conditions are:

(8.1.1) $\dfrac{\partial G_1}{\partial L_i} \leqslant 0$

(8.1.2) $\dfrac{\partial G_1}{\partial L_i} \cdot L_i = 0, i = i, \ldots, N$

(8.2.1) $\dfrac{\partial G_1}{\partial \gamma_i} \geqslant 0$

(8.2.2) $\dfrac{\partial G_1}{\partial \gamma_i} \gamma_i = 0, i = 1, \ldots, N$

(8.3) $\dfrac{\partial G_1}{\partial \lambda_{11}} = 0$

(8.4) $\dfrac{\partial G_1}{\partial \lambda_{12}} = 0.$

Differentiating (8) with respect to L_i we obtain:

(9) $L_i \cdot \dfrac{\partial G}{\partial L_i} = L_i[V_i(L_i)(1 + \eta_{V_i}) - \lambda_{11} +$

$$\lambda_{12}(\dfrac{\partial \mu_{p1}}{\partial L_i} + Z(\alpha)\dfrac{\partial \sigma_{p1}}{\partial L_i}) + \gamma_i] = 0$$

$$i = 1, \ldots, N$$

where $\eta_{V_i} = \dfrac{\partial V_i}{\partial L_i} \cdot \dfrac{L_i}{V_i} < 0.$

Two cases are of interest: (i) $L_i^* = 0$, which implies that borrower i does not receive the loan and $\gamma_i \geqslant 0$, (ii) $L_i^* \geqslant 0$, $\partial G/\partial L_i = 0$, which means that borrower i receives a positive loan. These implications are derived from the solution of the following equation:

(10) $V_i(1 + \eta_{V_i}) + \lambda_{12}(\dfrac{\partial \mu_{p1}}{\partial L_i} + Z(\alpha)\dfrac{\partial \sigma_{p1}}{\partial L_i}) = \lambda_{11} \equiv \dfrac{\partial G_1}{\partial \overline{K}}.$

$$i = 1, \ldots, N$$

(see Appendix 2A for exposition of $\dfrac{\partial \mu_{p1}}{\partial L_i}$ and $\dfrac{\partial \sigma_{p1}}{\partial L_i}$.)

The increase in the market value from relaxing the size constraint by one dollar is $\lambda_{11} \geqslant 0$; and λ_{12} is the shadow price of a dollar increment in equity (keeping $\overline{K}$ constant), or alternatively, the increase in the market value of the bank resulting from allowing higher risk on the credit portfolio.[12,13] Thus, the necessary condition for optimality for any two loans is:

$$(11) \quad \frac{\partial G}{\partial C} \equiv \lambda_{12} = \frac{V_i(1+\eta_{V_i}) - V_j(1+\eta_{V_j})}{\left(\frac{\partial \mu_{p1}}{\partial L_i} + Z(\alpha)\frac{\partial \sigma_{p1}}{\partial L_i} - \frac{\partial \mu_{p1}}{\partial L_j} - Z(\alpha)\frac{\partial \sigma_{p1}}{\partial L_j} \right)}$$

for all $i, j.$ $i \neq j.$

The difference in marginal returns from information of any two loans should be equal to the difference in their marginal effect on the safety-first constraint.

In order to further clarify the nature of equation (11), consider the case where increasing (issuing) equity capital does not involve transaction costs. In this case the safety-first constraint is not binding ($\lambda_{12} = 0$) and the bank maximizes its market value with limited financial sources and zero marginal costs. The necessary condition for market value maximization is the equality of the marginal returns from information of different loans (measured by λ_{11}). If it is further assumed that the bank has unlimited sources, then it can exploit all of its comparative advantage in producing services associated with loans, i.e., provide all loans with positive returns from information ($\lambda_{11} \geq 0$). The structure and the costs associated with the available financing sources are discussed in the next section (II.3).

D. Implications of the Credit Selection Model

Observe that the above model of credit allocation by commercial banks provides a basis for discussing several related topics, such as collateral considerations and bank-customer relationships.

First, note that the existence of collateral that is not part of the corporation's assets determines the loss distribution in case the firm goes bankrupt.[14] The bank's loss is reduced by the net sum of the realized collateral, whereas the borrower's loss is his equity plus the part of the collateral that covers its debt. Thus, the collateral can be considered a contingent claim sold (for the price of a reduction of the interest rate charged on the loan) to the bank by the borrower. As such, the collateral is traded at its market value and does not give a profit opportunity to the bank or to the borrower; however, it substantially reduces the effect of imperfect and asymmetric information about the borrower's activities.[15] Collateral reduces the demand for information about the borrower and, hence, the cost of borrowing. In a sense, the amount of collateral provided by a borrower reveals the firm's owners' expectations about their investments, thereby reducing the asymmetry of information. Alternatively, collateral can be viewed as a guarantee to assure the lender of the loan's quality. Finally, collateral affects the market value of the bank through its effect on the safety-first constraint. The impact of collateral on this constraint is determined primarily by the correlations among the returns on the different projects as well as the expected realized value of the collateral in the bank portfolio.

The role of customer-bank relationships has been analyzed by Hodgman (1963), Luckett (1970), and Black (1975). These works emphasize the importance of bank regulation in determining the form of such relations, apparent, for example, in such measures as "prime rate" and "compensating balances requirements" (which are, according to these works, merely a response to the interest rate ceilings on deposits). Because of uncertainty the high cost of information, bank-customer relationships play an important role in an *unregulated* market for banking services as well. In a loan market characterized by uncertainty, the (almost) cost-free access to information about customers provides banks with comparative advantages in producing financial services and presumably reduces interest rates charged on loans; hence, banks prefer depositors as loan customers rather than other borrowers, *cet. par.*[16]

II.3 The Bank Financing Decision and Liquidity Management

The liabilities of commercial banks consist of deposits, purchased funds, and equity capital. The structure of the market for these sources of funds, the nature of liquidity risk, and the bank's optimal financial structure are analyzed in this section.

A. The Structure of the Sources of Funds (Liabilities) Markets

1. Deposits

The deposit market consists of banks and depositors, both individuals and corporations. Deposits accounts reflect two separate dimensions: first, depositors' demands for bank services, and second, an investment vehicle for depositors (supply of funds to the bank). The demand for bank services as a medium for depositors' transactions (cash flows) differs among individuals and is determined by the expected reduction in transaction costs relative to other media of exchange in the economy. At the same time, the amounts (balances) held by depositors in their accounts provide the bank with a source of funds for its operations. In principle, the demand for bank services is separate from the funds provided. The depositors can hold most of their wealth in other financial assets and still use their accounts for a large volume of transactions. Because of the relatively high transaction costs (e.g., commissions, time consumption) associated with the conversion of financial assets, however, the demand for banks' services and the amount of deposits (supply of funds by depositors) are interrelated. The portion of customers' wealth held in deposits is a function of the differential rates of return on various financial assets, the cost of conversion of financial assets, and how intensively the bank is used as a medium for depositors' transactions. Other things equal, it is reasonable to assume that the larger the demand for bank services, the larger the average amount of deposits held in accounts. Accordingly, the demand for the two is interrelated. The supply (production) of these two goods is a separable process. Services could be charged under competition according to the marginal cost of producing them, and deposits could be paid the market rate of the financial assets they provide; however, the uncertainty regarding the characteristics of the financial asset (deposits) being traded affects the nature of the equilibrium in this market.

Uncertainty exists with respect to the properties ("quality") of deposits as financial assets. The bank is assumed *cet. par.* to prefer large deposits of long duration because of the transaction costs associated with acquiring or investing liquid assets. The quality, (i.e., the average amount and maturity) of each deposit account, however, is not fully known in advance. Furthermore, since the costs of evaluating and pricing each account (especially information costs or the costs of providing a schedule of interest rates for different maturities or different depositors) are relatively high (per dollar) for personal deposits, banks are assumed to pool all depositors and offer the same interest rate regardless of their quality (this assumption will be relaxed later). Under such market conditions, the high-quality depositors are under-rewarded and have incentives to hold other financial assets as investments. Therefore, given the transaction costs of transferring funds, they transfer the minimum amount required to their deposit accounts to cover the balances required for transactions or, alternatively, use other media of exchange (e.g., cash money). Accordingly, the lower return offered to high quality depositors causes a reduction in both the quality of deposits and in the total real amount of deposits,[17] (i.e., the low quality depositors "cause" external diseconomies). It is shown in the sequel that these features of the deposit market provide an explanation for several related practices: charging depositors less than the marginal cost of producing services, offering depositors different interest rates on time and demand deposits, and paying higher interest rates on large account balances.

The prevailing approach in the banking literature is to explain the practice of providing "subsidized" services to holders of demand deposits as a response to regulation (see e.g., Klein, 1971, and Black, 1975). The Banking Act of 1933 prohibits banks from paying an explicit interest rate on demand deposits. Thus, it is argued that depositors are paid indirectly by reducing the charges banks impose for administering the transaction mechanism below the cost of producing these services. Given the characteristics of the deposit market, however, this behavior can be expected from rational unregulated banks as well, i.e., the bank and the depositors prefer the pricing of the deposits and the transaction services as a bundle. Under the assumption that the scale of services demanded by depositors and the quality of depositors are closely related, such a package is an effective tool for screening the quality of depositors. For example, high quality depositors who are also assumed to have a relatively large number of transactions will be compensated (paid) by having their charges reduced according to the quality of their accounts. Two other explanations for such practices also may be delineated. First, the transaction costs involved in monitoring and the accounting system required for determining the explicit charge of each service and deposit account may prevent a completely separated pricing system from being cost-effective (see Benston and Smith, 1976). Second, tax considerations may play a role; since the interest received by depositors is taxable, whereas service cost payments on personal accounts are not tax-deductible, the bundling (offsetting) pricing method reduces tax payments by depositors and therefore is preferred.

The empirical evidence supports the argument that bundling charges for banks' products result from rational wealth maximization behavior on the part of banks and are not necessarily due to regulatory intervention. As noted by Benston and Smith (1976) (in the U.S.) "before the prohibition of interest payments on demand deposits (in 1933), banks generally paid interest only on large account balances and generally did not charge for individual services rendered." (P. 225, footnote 25.) In addition, the fact that other countries (Israel, Germany) do not have similar prohibition on interest payments, but nevertheless, use a bundling (packaging) pricing system, supports the above argument.

It should be noted that if the assumption about a close relationship between deposit balances and the demand for transactions services is not valid, then the bundling pricing system is inefficient since the reduction in depositors' transaction costs is less than the marginal cost of producing these services. This inefficiency should be compared with the advantages stated above in order to determine which charging system is preferable.

As indicated earlier, deposits can be screened (differentiated) by offering a schedule of contracts for various amounts and maturities. Such a practice, however, is very costly. Banks can still offer a smaller set of contracts in order to screen the polar deposits with extreme quality. The various types of time deposits are examples of such contracts, since they specify the quality of the deposits and the interest rate is paid accordingly. Thus, the interest rate differential on time and demand deposits is not necessarily attributed to reserve requirements or to the term structure of interest rates; rather it reflects the market's ability to screen their quality according to their maturity (probability of withdrawal).

Finally, it pays the bank to screen the quality of demand deposits of corporations with large account balances. As a result of economies of scale the bank can acquire information or write contracts that specify the quality of the deposit and, thus, pay interest (implicitly or explicitly) accordingly. For the purpose of this study, the following assumptions are made about the deposit market as a source of funds to the bank. It is assumed that the deposit market is competitive and efficient and provides no opportunities to make above-normal returns.[18] It is further assumed that balances are determined by the public's inelastic demand for transaction services. Therefore, the amount of real deposits is exogenously determined and is not a decision variable.[19]

2. Purchased Funds

The development of the money market during the 1960s led banks (especially large ones) to operate on the premise that, within relatively wide limits, additional funds can be invested or acquired at any time as long as the market rate of interest is met. The money market can be used to handle demand and supply of very large amounts, particularly for relatively short periods. The liabilities of financial institutions that suit this approach include large negotiable certificates of deposit, federal funds, Eurodollar loans, capital notes, and loans from the Federal Reserve. Money market borrowing and lending takes place mainly because the distribution of lending opportunities differs from the distribution of bank deposits. Even though marketable instruments differ slightly with respect to terms to maturity, interest rates, reserve requirements and availability, they are treated here as a homogenous unit.

Since there are many participants in this market, it is reasonable to assume that the market is quite efficient (i.e., borrowing or lending *per se* do not give rise to abnormal returns). Borrowing in this market involves transaction costs such as screening and contracting. These costs are relatively small; however, as the borrowed amounts increase, the marginal transaction costs also increase because of the costs of monitoring and searching.

3. Equity Capital

Capital markets are assumed to be efficient, i.e, there are no opportunities to make above-normal returns. Smith (1977) provides evidence about the magnitude of the transaction costs involved in raising additional equity capital. For issues using the underwriting method (which include about ninety percent of all issues), flotation costs averaged 6.17 percent of the proceeds but there were considerable economies of scale. Therefore, it is assumed that the marginal transaction costs associated with issuing capital are positive and greater than the marginal costs associated with money market borrowing within the relevant range, with a negative second derivative with respect to the amount raised.

The available sources of funds, particularly money market borrowing and financing policy, are integral parts of a commercial bank's liquidity management. The following subsection discusses the nature of liquidity risk and liquidity policies in commercial banks.

B. Liquidity Management in Commercial Banks

The importance of liquidity management is apparent from the involvement of commercial banks in intermediation between economic agents who wish to carry out transactions of different amounts and durations. For simplicity, let us assume that household savings (public deposits) are the principal source of external financing supply, and that bank credit is demanded solely by firms. A problem arises from the fact that deposits are liquid since they may be withdrawn at any point in time (even though the depositors may be subject to a fine or foregone interest), whereas loans are not liquid, since they cannot be realized before maturity.[20]

The difference between the timing of probable realization of a bank's assets and the possible withdrawal of its resources leads the commercial bank to hold sufficient liquid assets in order to meet unexpected deposit withdrawals (particularly those resulting from a negative money supply growth). It should be pointed out that the methods by which U.S. banks have been expected to meet such withdrawals have changed dramatically over time.[21] From the end of World War II until the beginning of the 1960s, the principal accepted practice was to hold highly liquid (marketable) reserves. During this period the Federal Reserve followed a policy of pegging interest rates on government bonds by offering to purchase or sell these securities at a set price. Thus, U.S. government securities were the main source of liquid reserves and constituted about 55 percent of the total assets of the banking system during the 1940s and 1950s.[22]

In the late 1950s the Federal Reserve changed its policy and allowed interest rates on government bonds to float. Thus, government securities became subject to the risk of unexpected changes in interest rates, especially as a result of monetary policy. Commercial banks did, in fact, suffer heavy capital losses during the 1950s because of the increase in market interest rates. This change in the nature of government securities policy induced commercial banks to adjust their liquidity management by reducing substantially their holdings of government bonds.

The so-called "liability management" approach to liquidity management was developed during the 1960s. Under this approach, whenever a bank experienced a reserve deficiency, funds were borrowed or purchased in the money market. The change resulting from this approach in the composition of banks' assets and liabilities was dramatic. At the beginning of the 1960s, liabilities of commercial banks consisted primarily of equity capital and public deposits. In contrast, at the present time, purchased funds make up about 16 percent of total bank liabilities and there has been a significant shift from liquid assets (primary and secondary reserves) to non-liquid assets (loans). The proportion of liquid to total assets was approximately 40 percent during the

1960s but fell to about 10 percent during the 1970s. In flow terms, this means that about 40 to 50 percent of the new money raised in recent years has come from interest sensitive purchased funds.

Under current practices commercial banks are expected to meet unexpected deposit withdrawals by using cash balances, borrowing in the money market or by selling securities. Holding currency has a negative net present value in terms of explicit opportunity costs, since it pays no interest. On the other hand, no transaction costs are involved in using currency to meet deposit withdrawals, Government securities are traded in an efficient market and incur relatively small transaction costs only when purchased or sold. The liability management practice allows banks to purchase funds in the money market whenever they experience demand for liquid assets. Under this practice liquidity is freely available but is subject to transaction costs, as discussed earlier.

Actually, liquidity management should consider all these possibilities for maximizing the market value of the bank. An optimal policy should consider a compendium of these alternatives according to their properties and to the stochastic nature of deposits flow. For the purpose of the present study, however, it is assumed that the liability management practice is the only strategy used to meet liquidity deficiency, i.e., deposit changes are matched by borrowing or lending in the money market.[23]

Finally, liquidity policy has an important impact on a bank's probability of failure, i.e., on the safety-first constraint. The impact on the safety-first constraint of borrowing in the money market is a function of expectations about deposit flows, the price fluctuations of money market funds, and the correlation between the two.[24] Since interest rates in the money market are highly sensitive to daily changes in demand and supply, the cost of replenishing liquidity deficiencies through this market is subject to frequent random fluctuations.[25]

C. A Model of a Bank's Financing Decision

This model discusses the bank's financing policy.

1. Assumptions

First, to focus attention on the financing decision, it is assumed that loans are homogeneous and all loans carry the same returns from information per dollar, the same probability of bankruptcy, and the same market interest rates. Further, their supply is perfectly elastic, and the returns on different loans are independent and uncorrelated with money market rates and deposits flows. In addition, loans are demanded (and granted) only at the beginning of the period during which they are illiquid.[26] The interest rate on loans is fixed and predetermined. Second, withdrawable deposits yield a fixed interest rate, assumed to be zero for simplicity. Deposits fluctuations reflect the behavior of the bank's depositors; hence, it is assumed that there is a negative covariability between the inflow of deposits to the bank and the market price of purchased money. Third, the interest rate on money market purchased funds is a function of the market, and is subject to frequent fluctuations. Borrowing in the money market involves low transaction costs per dollar (relative to equity capital), with increasing marginal cost as the amount borrowed increases. Fourth, issuing equity capital involves relatively high transaction costs with decreasing marginal cost. Fifth, it is assumed that during this period the bank is unable either to raise new equity capital or to grant new loans; hence, deposit changes during this period are matched by borrowing or lending in the money market.

Definitions and Notations:

$\overline{r}$ the interest factor charged on the loans, net of operating costs, for period 1;

$\overline{V}$ returns from information per dollar of loan, L;

D_t withdrawable deposits which bear zero interest,

$$D_t = \sum_{m=1}^{M} D_m, \qquad t = 0,1;$$

τ_1 the stochastic public deposit inflow during period 1 (assumed to take place at the beginning of the period). This random variable with a density function f is defined in the interval $-D_0$, D^u_1, where D^u_1 is the upper possible volume of deposits inflow. The vector of mean $E(\tau_1)$ and variance $V(\tau_1)$ fully defines f;

i_f the interest rate paid on purchased funds (F) during period 1, a random variable with density function g, distributed log normally with given parameters, mean $E(i_f)$ and variance $V(i_f)$;

$\text{Cov}(\tau_1, i_f)$ The covariability of deposits inflow ($E(\tau_1) > 0$) and the money market rate of interest. $\text{Cov}(\tau_1, i_f) < 0$ (see assumption 3).

$\beta(F_0)$ The impact of the amount borrowed on the interest rate determined by the market (for a given investment policy) where $\beta'(F_0) \geqslant 0$ $\beta(F_0) = 1$ for $F_0 \leqslant 0$.

$T_2(F_0)$ the transaction costs associated with borrowing at the money market, where $T_2'(F_0) > 0$ and $T_2''(F_0) \geqslant 0$; and

$T_1(C)$ the transaction costs associated with issuing equity capital.
$T_1'(C)>0$ $T_1''(C) \leqslant 0$ and $T_1'(C) > T_2'(F_0)$ within the relevant range.

Thus, the model is a single period market value maximization model. The bank decides on the optimal amount of borrowing and equity capital at the present, knowing that before the end of the planning period public deposits and money market rates may change. Formally, the bank is looking for an optimal amount of loans and composition of equity capital and purchased funds so as to

(12)   Maximize $(MV - C) = L\bar{V} - T_1(C) - T_2(F_0) \int_{-D_0}^{F_0} (F_0 - \tau_1) f(\tau_1) d(\tau_1)$

S.t

(12.1) $F_t + D_t + C = L$

(12.2) $\mu_{p2} + Z(\alpha) \sigma_{p2} = -C$

where:

(13) $\mu_{p2} = L[\bar{r}(1 - \bar{P}) - 1] - F_0 \beta(F_0) E(i_f) + \beta(F_0) E(\tau_1 i_f)$

(14) $\sigma_{p2} = [L^2 \bar{r}^2 \bar{P}(1 - \bar{P}) + F_0^2 \beta(F_0)^2 V(i_f)$

$+ \beta(F_0)^2 V(\tau_1 i_f) - F_0 \beta(F_0)^2 \text{cov}(i_f, \tau_1 i_f)]^{1/2}.$

Define the Lagrangian function $G_2 = G_2(L, C, F_0, \lambda_{21}, \lambda_{22})$:

(15) $G_2 = L \cdot \bar{V} - T_1(C) - T_2(F_0) \int_{-D_0}^{F_0} (F_0 - \tau_1) f(\tau_1) d(\tau_1) +$

$\lambda_{21}(C + D_0 + F_0 - L) + \lambda_{22}(\mu_{p2} + Z(\alpha) \sigma_{p2} + C).$

Differentiating (15), and setting

$$\frac{\partial G_2}{\partial L}, \frac{\partial G_2}{\partial C}, \frac{\partial G_2}{\partial F_0}, \frac{\partial G_2}{\partial \lambda_{21}}, \frac{\partial G_2}{\partial \lambda_{22}},$$

equal to zero, the necessary conditions for a maximum are obtained:

(16.1) $\dfrac{\partial G_2}{\partial L} = \bar{V} - \lambda_{21} + \lambda_{22}(\dfrac{\partial \mu_{p2}}{\partial L} + Z(\alpha)\dfrac{\partial \sigma_{p2}}{\partial L}) = 0$

(16.2) $\dfrac{\partial G_2}{\partial F_0} = -T_2'(F_0) \int_{-D_0}^{F_0} (F_0 - \tau_1) f(\tau_1) d(\tau_1) -$

$$T_2(F_0)\int_{-D_0}^{F_0} f(\tau_1)d(\tau_1) + \lambda_{21} + \lambda_{22}(\frac{\partial \mu_{p2}}{\partial F_0} + Z(\alpha)\frac{\partial \sigma_{p2}}{\partial F_0}) = 0.[27]$$

(16.3) $\dfrac{\partial G_2}{\partial C} = -T_1'(C) + \lambda_{21} + \lambda_{22} = 0$

(16.4) $\dfrac{\partial G_2}{\partial \lambda_{21}} = C + D_0 + F_0 - L = 0$

(16.5) $\dfrac{\partial G_2}{\partial \lambda_{22}} = \mu_{p2} + Z(\alpha)\sigma_{p2} + C = 0.$

The marginal increase in the bank's market value resulting from an increase in the size of the bank is λ_{21}. A necessary condition for optimum is that the marginal costs of the various sources be equal to the increase in the market value due to their use.

(17.1) equity capital fixed: $\overline{V} + \lambda_{22}(\dfrac{\partial \mu_{p2}}{\partial L} + Z(\alpha)\dfrac{\partial \sigma_{p2}}{\partial L})$

$$= T_2'(F_0)\int_{-D_0}^{F_0}(F_0 - \tau_1)f(\tau_1)d(\tau_1) + T_2(F_0)\int_{-D_0}^{F_0} f(\tau_1)d(\tau_1) -$$

$$\lambda_{22}(\dfrac{\partial \mu_{p2}}{\partial F_0} + Z(\alpha)\dfrac{\partial \sigma_{p2}}{\partial F_0})$$

(17.2) borrowed funds fixed:

$$\overline{V} + \lambda_{22}(\dfrac{\partial \mu_{p2}}{\partial L} + Z(\alpha)\dfrac{\partial \sigma_{p2}}{\partial L} + 1) = T_1'(C).$$

The optimality conditions (17) state that the difference between returns from information on loans and the transaction costs of issuing claims should equal the change in market value caused by the change in the probability of bankruptcy. For example, increasing equity capital involves transaction costs $T_1'(C)$ and benefits the bank both as a source of funds (λ_{21}) and as a factor which reduces the probability of bankruptcy (λ_{22}). The value of this function is endogenously determined by the borrowing and lending opportunities. For example:

(18) $\lambda_{22} = \dfrac{T_1'(C) - \overline{V}}{\dfrac{\partial \mu_{p2}}{\partial L} + Z(\alpha)\dfrac{\partial \sigma_{p2}}{\partial L} + 1}.$

To the extent that issuing an additional dollar of equity capital and granting the proceeds as a loan decreases the probability of bank failure, the bank is willing to accept a negative margin $[T_i{}'(C) - \overline{V}]$ on the transaction. Finally, although deposits are assumed as given, they play an important role in the financing decision through their interactions with other issued claims. Changes in the initial level of deposits (D_0) affect the solution obtained through the effect of deposits on the expected distribution of deposit withdrawals and the covariability with the money market interest rate. Let us assume that an increase in current deposits reflects greater diversification among depositors and economic areas. Therefore, the increase in current public deposits is expected to reduce the covariability between deposit flows and money market interest rate changes (i.e., the bank is less exposed to unexpected changes in money market interest rate fluctuations). Hence it reduces the impact on the probability of bankruptcy due to increased borrowing from the money market.

In summary, this section discussed the financing policy of commercial banks. The essence of a bank's financing management is the decision as to the type and volume of financial claims to issue. Three types of claims were considered: deposits, which are an integral part of the transaction services provided by banks; equity capital, which is relatively costly and infrequently issued in comparison to other sources; and borrowing in the money market, which provides the bank an unlimited short-term borrowing opportunity that is risky because of liquidity considerations. Emphasis was placed on the cost involved in issuing each type of claim and on the interactions between the financing and the investment (credit) decisions.

II.4   A Theory of a Bank's Decision-Making Process

This section extends the analysis of the investment and financing decisions and combines them in order to provide a more unified theory of the decision-making process of an individual bank. The interaction between the investment decision and the financing decision is of importance in determining the optimal composition of assets and liabilities; in particular, it has an additional important dimension because of the safety-first constraint.

A.   The Investment Decision

The demand for a loan by a single borrower provides the bank with a downward sloping schedule of marginal returns from information as the amount of a loan increases. In addition, each loan affects the bank's probability of bankruptcy, and hence, the bank's market value. The magnitude of this effect is endogenously determined by the set of other loans granted, by the bank's financing structure, and by the safety-first constraint. Therefore, the schedule of the marginal increase in the bank's market value provided by the amount loaned to any single borrower is an integral part of the solution to the maximization problem. For any given amount of loan portfolio, ($\bar{K}$), and a given structure of financing sources, the optimal amount granted to each borrower can be derived using equation (10) in section II.2. By varying the size of the loan portfolio and keeping the ratio of capital-to-borrowed funds constant, the schedule of marginal returns for each loan is ($MR\ L_i$) and the aggregate returns for the credit portfolio is ($MR\ \sum\limits_{i}^{N} L_i$). Observe that because of the safety-first constraint, the schedule of returns is determined by the interaction between the loans and the financial structure. In Figure 2-2, for example, three loan opportunities are considered. In the initial state, the amount $\bar{K}_0$ is allocated among these loans and the optimal amount of loans (L_i^{0*}) is derived. The solution also provides the shadow price of an additional dollar (λ_{11}), i.e., the largest return on a dollar of a rejected loan. Since returns from information in the loan market are limited, an increase in the amount of sources available from $\bar{K}_0$ to $\bar{K}_1$ decreases accordingly the shadow price of an additional dollar from λ^0_{11} to λ^1_{11} and the optimal loan amounts L_i^{1*} rise.

B. The Financing Decision

Changes in the financial structure, for a given amount of loan portfolio, result in a shift of the marginal returns schedule of each loan and, hence, in the optimal amount of loans. For example, an increase in equity capital for any size of loan portfolio will shift the aggregate returns curve on loans (and will also affect the individual loan's profit schedule) above and to the right since the shadow price of the safety-first constraint is reduced. In Figure 2-3, for example, an increase in equity capital from C_0 to C_1 increases the marginal returns opportunities from λ^0_{11} to λ^1_{11}. The upper limit of these changes is the aggregate returns from the loan opportunities schedule for that amount of capital on which the safety-first constraint is not binding, or at the extreme, when equity capital is the only source of financing ($C_2 = \bar{K}$). On the upper limit curve (i.e., where the safety-first constraint is not binding at $C_2 = \bar{K}$), the returns from information on different loans are *independent of each other*. The aggregate returns-from-information curve of the credit portfolio is simply a horizontal summation of the individual curves and is not determined by the solution to the optimization problem.

C. The Individual Bank's Decision-Making Process

The analysis of the investment policy in this section assumes a given financial structure, and also considers the effect of changes in the structure of liabilities

Figure 2-2

The Investment Decision

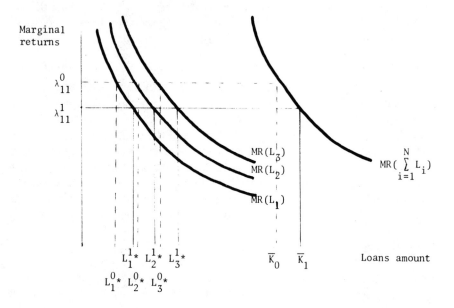

Figure 2-3

The Effect of Financial Structure on Investment Opportunities

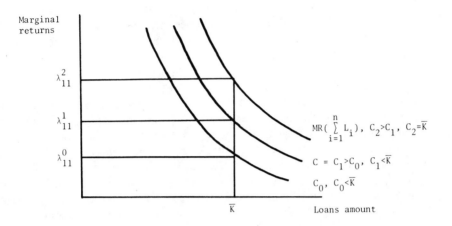

on the optimal credit portfolio through the safety-first constraint. This analysis, however, ignores the cost associated with each composition of liabilities, and therefore, does not provide an optimal financing policy.

The marginal cost of both equity capital and borrowed funds includes transaction costs (independent of each other) and costs (benefits for equity capital) associated with their impact on the safety-first constraint (the latter depends on the loans and on other liabilities the bank holds). Therefore, the schedule of the marginal costs of equity capital and borrowed funds for various sizes of loan portfolios is derived, along with the optimal size of each loan, from the maximization problem analyzed in Appendix 2B.[28]

For any given amount of credit portfolio ($\bar{K}$) in Figure 2-4, the marginal returns from information (increase in the bank's market value) MR, and the marginal cost (above the financial market equilibrium), MC, are determined and the difference between the two represents the profit opportunities of a dollar increase in the size of the bank. By varying the size of the credit portfolio, the schedule of the marginal costs of the different sources and the marginal returns from information of each loan can be derived.[29] An increase in the size of the bank from $\bar{K}_0$ to $\bar{K}_1$ reduces the marginal returns in the loan market from MR^0 to MR^1 and increases the marginal costs of issuing claims from MC^0 to MC^1. The amount of loans that exploits all profit opportunities in the different markets is the optimal size of the credit portfolio ($\bar{K}^* = L^*$). The optimality conditions (see Appendix 2B) state that the marginal returns from any two loans ($\lambda^*_{31} = MR_i^*$) should be the same, and equal to the marginal costs of acquiring both equity capital and borrowed funds ($\lambda^*_{31} = MC^*$). The marginal returns from information on a dollar of loan should exactly offset the marginal cost of acquiring an additional dollar. Therefore, the optimal size of the bank is determined by the returns from information in the loan markets, the costs associated with issuing different claims, and the interaction between them, given the safety-first constraint.

The decrease in the market value from the safety-first constraint is a function of the available set of returns from information on loans and the transaction costs associated with issuing claims. As discussed earlier, the solution obtained in Appendix 2B will lead to market value maximization only if α is set so that it reduces the market value (compared with no restriction) by the same amount as the expected costs of bankruptcy.

Finally, a decrease in the imposed probability of bankruptcy (i.e., increasing the absolute value of $Z(\alpha)$ in the chance constraint) affects both the financing and investment decisions of the commercial bank as discussed in section III.2.

The decision-making processes of unregulated banks discussed in this chapter provide useful insights into the economic role of banks under uncertainty. The rationale of adopting new practices in banking as well as their

Figure 2-4

The Decision-Making Process

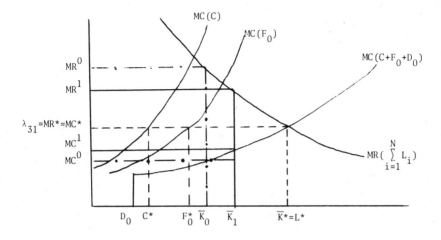

expected impact on the banks' market value maximization processes can be analyzed within the context of the above discussion. Also, the unified theory of the decision-making process provides a general framework for analyzing the impact of different regulatory schemes on banks' market values and the social costs involved in their implementation.

Chapter III

An Analysis of the Banking Industry Under Capital Adequacy Regulation

The financial intermediation system in most countries is subject to government intervention. Therefore, the normative model of the individual bank decision-making process was developed in the previous chapter to form a basis for analyzing the banking industry under capital adequacy regulation. Portfolio constraints and other means used by different countries to constrain the risk of bank failures and protect the depositors are examined, and the decision-making processes of banks under different regulations are considered. Attention is focused on changes induced in the composition of bank assets and liabilities and on possible adverse effects (as opposed to the intended effects) that increase the probability of bank failures. Subsequently, the social and private costs of regulatory constraints on bank decision-making and on the costs of regulation are discussed and the efficiency of different sets of regulations in terms of their social costs is evaluated. Finally, an alternative approach to bank regulation is suggested that is likely to increase social welfare.

In essence, the analysis suggests that: 1) regulation constraints and other means used in different countries could lead to adverse effects on the probability of bank failures; 2) the current bank regulation process is not efficient and involves higher social costs than alternative regulatory schemes; and 3) the ineffectiveness and inefficiency of bank regulation in different countries call for reconsideration of existing regulatory systems and for suggestions for their improvement.

III.1 Capital Adequacy Regulations

Alternative economic rationales for bank regulation have been examined in several studies (for example, Meltzer, 1967; Benston, 1973; Black, Miller, Posner, 1978). These studies suggest that the explanations that have a sound economic foundation and are supported by evidence are: (i) the existence of deficiencies in information, i.e., banks' customers operate with a high degree of ignorance as to the banks' degrees of riskiness; and (ii) external diseconomies associated with the impact of the bankruptcy of a single bank on the public's confidence in the banking system as a whole. Based on these arguments and according to what regulators claim they are doing, it is hypothesized that capital adequacy regulation is demanded by consumers of banking services and is intended to protect depositors and to prevent bank failures (in the U.S. to protect the FDIC's funds).[1] Different countries use bank regulations in various ways to achieve their goals. This section discusses three major means of regulation: (A) portfolio (solvency) constraints, (B) bank examination, and (C) deposit insurance.

A. Portfolio (Solvency) Constraints

Current bank regulations may be classified into the following general types of constraints: licensing, pricing, and portfolio. Licensing and pricing constraints primarily determine the environment and the market structure (competition) for banking services. Portfolio constraints restrict the freedom of an individual bank to engage in risky activities or to hold a high-risk portfolio of assets and liabilities. This study is concerned mainly with the portfolio constraints that are generally called capital adequacy regulation.

Black, et. al., (1978) point out that portfolio constraints on banks' decision-making processes are similar to those imposed by private lenders. In banking, however, in addition to the variance-risk involved in the investment and financing decisions, there are other types of risk stemming from the very nature of banking operations, namely those incurred in the intermediation between sources and uses. Commercial banks specialize in certain assets and liabilities markets, and these assets and liabilities may differ as to terms of maturity, currency of denomination, etc., which leads to intermediation risks.

The analysis of the portfolio constraints presented in this section has particular reference to the regulatory laws currently in force in 27 countries (a detailed list is provided later). The specific legal requirements of each country surveyed, however, are not detailed here. Rather the study attempts to find elements common to the provisions in the various countries and to associate them with the different types of banking risk. In particular, four types of provisions are identified and discussed: 1) contraints on financing decisions; 2) constraints on investment decisions; 3) constraints on liquidity management; and 4) constraints on foreign exchange operations.

1. Constraints on the Financing Decisions

The purpose of requirements related to a bank's financing decisions is to ensure the adjustment of capital size to an increase in the bank's activity (and external financing) and thereby to protect banks from bankruptcy in the event of earnings (or assets) problems. Three capital ratios are common: capital/public's deposits; capital/total liabilities; and capital/risky assets.[2] The first two indices are general and do not refer to the different degrees of risk involved in different operations and assets. The third index is aimed more directly at relating capital to those assets that are likely to require a buffer against unforeseen losses. The leverage size determines the riskiness of different claims issued by the bank as well as the probability of bankruptcy. An increase in the equity capital of a bank reduces the risk to its creditors, particularly depositors. The larger the ratio of the bank's equity capital to total assets, the less are stockholder's investment incentives (moral hazards) to increase the variance-risk of the bank.

2. Constraints on the Investment Decisions

The largest portion of the regulatory authorities' efforts is devoted to an evaluation of the bank's loans (investments).

It is difficult and costly to impose a direct constraint on the composition of the asset portfolio a bank is allowed to hold; however, a regulator can impose a general constraint both on the minimum degree of asset diversification and on activities that banks can pursue. Increased diversification is desirable since it lowers the incentives for fraud and reduces the probability of bankruptcy (see Jaffee and Russell, 1976). Bankruptcy is less probable because returns from investments in different types of loans are likely to be imperfectly correlated.[3] Regulatory authorities in some countries impose separate control on certain types of assets, e.g., loans to directors, managers, and companies connected with the bank. These considerations give rise to legal requirements concerning (a) a ceiling on the size of any single asset in the bank portfolio ("size constraint"), and (b) the kind of assets banks are allowed to hold ("the activity constraint").

a. Size Constraints—Ceiling on Loans to Any Single Borrower as a Percentage of Equity Capital

Restrictions of this type exist in most countries (21 out of the 27 studied). The percentages range from 10 to 40 percent of the bank's capital. Controls in the various countries range from reporting of the extension of large credit (Luxemburg, United Kingdom) to certain rigid constraints that prevent concentration of risk (Germany). This restriction is of a general nature; collateral provided by borrowers is not considered nor is an efficient allocation of credit among projects assured. The restrictions rule out, however, the possibility of having a portfolio that is heavily weighted with one type of risky loan; i.e., it prevents the possibility that a single borrower's bankruptcy would lead to a bank's failure.

Ceiling on Loans to Interested Parties as a Percentage of Equity Capital: This restriction reflects the high risk involved in loans of this type. Such loans reduce the diversification of the credit portfolio and may not be the result of a strictly commercial ("arm's length") transaction.[4] Generally, regulatory authorities in some countries impose more restrictive constraints on loans to managers and directors relative to the general size constraint. For example, in the Netherlands a borrower's risky assets (loans) normally may not exceed 25 percent of equity capital, and advances to *all* directors, managers, and other associated borrowers may not exceed 2 percent of equity capital. Belgian law, as another example, requires a 100 percent equity capital cover for such loans in addition to the usual requirements regarding the capital-to-risky assets ratio, indicating that authorities regard these kinds of loans as absolute risks.

Ceiling on Investments in and Loans to Subsidiary Companies (Including Banks) as a Percentage of Equity Capital: This type of restriction prevents the allocation of large sums to a single investment (increases diversification). It also restricts investments in organizations, such as subsidiaries of bank holding companies, that would maximize the market value of the holding company possibly at the expense of the subsidiary bank's creditors (depositors and the FDIC). This issue is discussed further in Chapter IV.

b. Activity Constraint—Restrictions on the Type of Business Banks Can Undertake

This restriction prohibits banks from engaging in certain types of activities, such as holding stock in other companies. The provision also may prevent banks from expanding into nonbank activities that might involve higher risks than banking. In most countries, the restriction limits banks to banking activities only. However, authorities have considerable latitude in deciding what is, and what is not, a permissible activity. The list of permissible activities varies across countries and over time in each country (the attitude of regulators in the United States is discussed in Chapter IV).

3. Constraints on Liquidity Management

Two requirements can be distinguished. First, *capital must cover fixed assets.* Equity capital serves as a tool for maintaining equilibrium between the maturities of assets and liabilities (liquidity). In banking, a fixed asset is used for the production of banking services, and thus usually will not be sold as long as the bank is a going concern. Therefore, fixed assets are not available to meet cash outflow. Accordingly, capital available to maintain an adjustment between the maturity of assets and liabilities is reduced by the amount invested in fixed assets. In England and Ireland, for example, evaluation of bank capital adequacy ratios is based upon the amount of "free capital," which is defined as equity capital *less* buildings, equipment, commercial investments, and goodwill. In other countries (e.g., Belgium, the Netherlands, Luxemburg, Germany) capital must cover the entire value of fixed assets.

A second requirement concerning liquidity is *required reserves.* In most countries reserve requirements are based on a percentage of deposits applied according to the maturity of the various deposits; the longer the repayment period, the lower the liquidity ratio. However, if the reserve requirements were to meet their presumed goals (i.e., reducing liquidity risk), they should be applied to assets as well as to liabilities as suggested in the model (section II.3) presented in the previous chapter. Clearly, liquidity problems in the banking industry are not the result only of the resource side, but also of the structure of the maturity dates of the assets and liabilities and, in particular, of the extent to which these dates coincide.

Although in some countries (Holland, Switzerland, and West Germany) the laws refer to the mutual relationship that should exist between the maturity dates of assets and liabilities (and, consequently, between capital and liquid assets), in most countries reserve requirements apply only to the resources side, and capital requirements completely ignore the liquidity risk. Also, in most countries the bank can use only a fraction (reserve ratio) of its required reserves to meet unexpected deposits and withdrawals.[5] Therefore, this constraint primarily affects the composition of the bank's asset portfolio rather than its liquidity position, i.e., liquid reserves are riskless assets.[6]

4. Constraints on Foreign Exchange Operations
Some countries, such as Holland, Switzerland, and West Germany, impose restrictions on uncovered positions of foreign currency as a percentage of equity capital. In most countries, however (e.g., Israel, Belgium, England), this regulation is within the government's general control of foreign currency.

5. Other Regulations
In addition to the laws reviewed above, the following regulations are imposed by various authorities: restrictions on the distribution of dividends (in most countries), restrictions on a single stockholder's bank shares (designed to prevent self-dealing and fraud); specifications as to the internal composition of capital (the proportion of debentures to total capital, in the United States), and a ceiling on the amount of any single deposit.[7,8]

In summary, regulators in different countries use similar portfolio constraints; however, regulations differ with respect to the composition and magnitude of the requirements and as to the legal form of regulation (by a law or specific requirements).[9]

Portfolio constraints in different countries can be classified into fairly homogenous groups:

Countries that Follow the British Legal Requirements: This group includes countries that have adopted the tradition of British bank supervision.[10] They have almost no portfolio constraints, but their supervisory institutions maintain continuous surveillance that makes use of a number of capital ratios. For the purpose of a final evaluation of capital adequacy, additional data, such as a bank's profitability and the nature of its management, are used.

South American and Asian Countries: All countries included in this group use legal requirements of uniformly high minimum capital ratios for all items of bank assets and ignore other types of risk.[11]

Western European Countries: In general, regulators in these countries use different capital ratios for different assets, and other (more complicated) requirements to relate capital size to risk in various banking operations.[12,13]

Enforcement of portfolio constraints is accomplished mainly through bank examination which is discussed below.

B. Bank Examination

The major tasks of bank examination are: first, to prevent bank failures caused by mismanagement and dishonesty; second, to acquire information regarding the adequacy of bank's capital, and, accordingly, to enforce capital requirements; and third, to ensure that laws regulating banking activities are being followed. U.S. bank failures before 1971 were more often the result of dishonesty, and self-serving employees and management than of incompetent management. Benston (1973, p. 40) found that fraud and other irregularities were the major cause of failure in two-thirds of the 56 banks that failed between 1959 and 1971. Loan losses from self-serving loans or brokered funds were the primary cause in another 25 percent of the failures. Inept management accounted for the remaining 7 percent. In these circumstances, portfolio constraints *per se* would not have been sufficient to prevent bank failure. More emphasis would have to be placed on fraud detection and on examination of internal control systems of banks.

Bank examination and portfolio constraints are complementary measures of capital adequacy regulation. Bank examination is directed mainly toward small banks where the internal control generally is inadequate and the potential for fraud and defalcation is greater. Larger banks where internal control is more efficient, on the other hand, are more likely to fail due to mismanagement. Although most U.S. bank failures in the past (1940-1971) have involved very small banks, there has been a trend in recent years toward progressively larger banks experiencing failure (see Horvitz, 1975). Therefore, the role of portfolio constraints and of other means of controlling the risk of bank failure deserves more attention today than in the past.

C. Deposit Insurance

In some countries, capital adequacy regulations are accomplished through mandatory government insurance and portfolio constraints.[14] In the United States, a constant rate insurance premium per dollar of domestic deposit is charged (whether covered by insurance or not).

Two basic purposes of deposit insurance are to protect depositors (up to a limit of $40,000 on an individual account) and to protect the banking system against destructive runs on deposits.[15] Deposit insurance eliminates the danger of loss for most depositors, thereby reducing the relatively high costs of information and surveillance that small depositors otherwise would incur.[16] Government guarantees for deposits can be provided because of economies of scale in information and monitoring costs and large-scale guarantees to the banking system (see Mayer, 1965; Kreps and Wacht, 1971; and Gibson, 1972). In addition, because of the protection these guarantees offer, depositors have no need to withdraw funds from insolvent banks, or from banks that they fear will become insolvent. Hence, runs on such banks are unlikely, and, in fact, have not occurred. Holders of deposits in excess of the $40,000 ceiling, however, partially bear the default risk and may tend to withdraw their funds, thereby adding to a bank's problem.[17] Finally, an important factor in determining the consequences of deposit insurance is the FDIC's policy at the time of bank failure. The FDIC can either provide assistance for purchase (merger into) by another bank or liquidate the failed bank.[18] This purchase and assumption transaction provides, in effect, 100 percent insurance to uninsured depositors. In fact, the nature of this regulation has been such that most deposits are 100 percent insured despite the official maximum on the amount of deposit insured.

In conclusion, various means are used by bank regulators of different countries to constrain the probability of bank failures and to protect depositors, and different constraints are used to control different types of risk. The following section will be a discussion of the combined effect of different sets of regulation.

III.2   The Decision-Making Process of Banks Under Capital Adequacy Regulations

The individual bank's decision-making process under regulatory constraints is considered in this section. The main emphasis is on the evaluation of the impact of bank regulation on a bank's overall variance-risk. First, the impact of an ideal "direct" chance constraint is analyzed to explore the consequences of intended bank regulation. Second, two alternative regulation sets are analyzed. In the first one, it is assumed that regulators impose a set of portfolio constraints similar to those used in different countries. In the second set, deposit insurance is added to the portfolio constraints.

The analysis suggests that the induced changes resulting from the set of portfolio constraints may lead to effects that are adverse to regulatory efforts, because they increase the probability of bank failure. Also, it will be shown that a bank's incentive to offset the regulatory efforts is even stronger under

regulations that include portfolio constraints and, in the United States, deposit
insurance.

A. The Individual Bank's Decision-Making Process Under a "Direct" Chance Constraint

The intended effects of bank regulation can best be analyzed by assuming that
regulators are able to specify, measure, and enforce a direct chance constraint
on the probability of bank failures. The implication of a direct chance
constraint can be examined by utilizing the model of individual bank decision-
making presented in the previous chapter. Denote α as the probability of
bankruptcy allowed by the regulatory constraint. If this constraint is not
binding (i.e., if the safety-first constraint the bank uses allows a lower
probability of bankruptcy), it is clear that regulation has no effect on an
individual bank's decision-making process. A binding constraint actually
causes an increase in the absolute value of $Z(\alpha)$ in the safety-first constraint,
i.e., a decrease in the rate of substitution between risk (variance) and return
(mean) in the bank's portfolio of assets and liabilities. Thus, the direct-chance
constraint is expected to affect the investment and financing decisions
undertaken by a bank.

Changes in the composition of assets and liabilities and in the optimal size
of the bank resulting from such constraints can be examined using comparative
statics analysis. Such comparative statics analysis that uses the model discussed
in section II.3 is presented in Appendix 3A. Loans are assumed to be
homogeneous and the marginal cost of issuing equity capital is constant. It is
shown that as the constrained probability of bank failure decreases (absolute
value of $Z(\alpha)$ increases), the amount of borrowed funds decreases
$dF_0/d|(Z(\alpha)|<0$; the shadow price of a dollar increment in loans decreases
$d\lambda_{21}/d|(Z(\alpha)|<0$; and the shadow price of the safety-first constraint increases
$d\lambda_{22}/d|(Z(\alpha)|>0$. The induced changes in the amount of loans granted $dL/d|(Z(\alpha)|$ and the size of equity capital $dC/d|(Z(\alpha)|$ cannot be determined *a
priori*. As indicated by the comparative statics analysis, their magnitudes
depend on the marginal contributions of loans versus borrowed funds to the
bank's overall variance-risk (safety-first constraint) and also on the change in
the marginal transaction costs of borrowed funds.

The important aspect of the direct chance constraint is the fact that the
induced change in the shadow price of risk taking (λ_{22}) equally affects all
decisions undertaken by banks.[19] For example, an increase in λ_{22} implies an
increase in the required return on loans and liabilities for a given level of risk.
Equivalently, the bank is forced to shift its financial structure toward more
equity capital and/or to reject (profitable) risky investments, in order to reduce
its probability of failure. In this sense, direct constraints control the bank's

overall risk and account for the interaction among the different decisions. Therefore, the direct chance constraint serves as a normative basis (i.e., the intended effects of regulation) for evaluating the effectiveness of the regulation sets currently in use.

B. The Individual Bank Decision-Making Process Under Portfolio Constraints

This section examines the effectiveness of a set of portfolio restrictions in constraining the risk of bank failures by considering the simultaneous impact of various portfolio constraints on a bank's composition of assets and liabilities and on its probability of bankruptcy. Attention is focused on possible adverse effects (as opposed to the intended effects) resulting from the interaction between different types of decision-making.

Three types of balance-sheet constraints that approximate regulations actually employed in different countries are considered explicitly in the model. Other regulations, implicit in the model, are also discussed in this section.

1. Constraint on the Investment Policy—Size Constraints
A ceiling equal to a specified percentage of equity capital is placed on loans to a single borrower. Mathematically, this constraint can be stated as $L_i \leqslant aC$ where $0 < a < 1$ is fixed by the regulator, (L_i = *loan*, C = *equity capital,* as defined by the regulator).

2. Constraint on Liquidity Management-Reserve Requirements
Reserve requirements force banks to invest a certain proportion of their funds in specific riskless assets. For simplicity it is assumed that the same percentage, h, applies to all deposits and money market funds. Furthermore, it is assumed that this constraint is binding. Therefore, $M = h(D_0 + F_0)$ where M denotes the riskless assets (for simplicity assumed as cash).

3. Constraint on Financing Policy—the Leverage Constraint
A constraint on financing policy would require banks to have relatively more equity capital than they would in the absence of such a constraint. The most general kind of capital constraint requires a bank to maintain at least a given ratio of equity capital to the sum of deposits and borrowed funds. Formally, this constraint can be stated as $C \geqslant b(F_0 + D_0)$, where $b > 0$ is fixed by the regulator. It is assumed that this constraint is binding, i.e., $C = b(F_0 + D_0)$.

Another restriction (the permissible activities) prohibits banks from engaging in certain types of business, such as the holding of equity securities of other companies.[20] This restriction limits the feasible set of investments. Moreover, the investment constraints (i.e., the amount of loans and the permissible activities) are likely to alter the bank-customer relationships and hence the available returns to information (V_i^*). This effect relates more closely to the social costs and efficiency of the regulatory process and will be discussed in the following section. Finally, it is assumed that the safety-first constraint is not binding as a result of the regulatory constraint.

The model of the individual bank's decision-making process developed in the previous chapter is used to analyze the effect of regulatory constraints on this process. The definitions of variables are the ones used earlier in section II.2 and II.3. Thus, a model is structured in which the bank wishes to find a vector $(L_1 L_2, \ldots, L_n, F_0)$ so as to:

$$(19) \quad \text{Maximize } (MV - C) = \sum_{i=1}^{N} L_i V_i^* - T_1[C = b(F_0 + D_0)] -$$

$$T_2(F_0) \int_{-D_0}^{F_0} (F_0 - \tau_1) f(\tau_1) d(\tau_1)$$

S.t.

(19.1) $L_i \geqslant 0 \quad i = 1, 2, \ldots, N$

(19.2) $L_i \leqslant aC = a \cdot b(F_0 + D_0) \quad i = 1, 2, \ldots, N$

$$(19.3) \quad \sum_{i=1}^{N} L_i = (F_0 + D_0)(1 + b - h)$$

Define $G_4 = G_4[L_i, \gamma_i, W_i, F_0, \lambda_{41}]$ such that

$$(20) \quad G_4 = \sum_{i=1}^{N} L_i V_i^* - T_1[b(F_0 + D_0)] -$$

$$T_2(F_0) \int_{-D_0}^{F_0} (F_0 - \tau_1) f(\tau_1) d(\tau_1) + \gamma_i L_i + W_i[a \cdot b(F_0 + D_0) - L_i] +$$

$$\lambda_{41}[(1 + b - h)(F_0 + D_0) - \sum_{i=1}^{N} L_i].$$

The necessary conditions for an optimum are:

(21.1.1) $\quad \dfrac{\partial G_4}{\partial L_i} \leqslant 0$

(21.1.2) $\quad \dfrac{\partial G_4}{\partial L_i} \cdot L_i = L_i[V_i^*(1 + \eta V_i^*) + \gamma_i - W_i - \lambda_{41}] = 0$

$\quad\quad\quad i = 1, 2, \ldots, N$

(21.2.1) $\quad \dfrac{\partial G_4}{\partial \gamma_i} \geqslant 0$

(21.2.2) $\quad \dfrac{\partial G_4}{\partial \gamma_i} \cdot \gamma_i = 0 \quad i = 1, \ldots, N$

(21.3.1) $\quad \dfrac{\partial G_4}{\partial W_i} \geqslant 0$

(21.3.2) $\quad \dfrac{\partial G_4}{\partial W_i} \cdot W_i = W_i[a \cdot b(F_0 + D_0) - L_i] = 0 \quad i = 1, \ldots, N$

(21.4) $\quad \dfrac{\partial G_4}{\partial F_0} = -bT_1'(C) - T_2'(F_0) \displaystyle\int_{-D_0}^{F_0} (F_0 - \tau_1) f(\tau_1) d(\tau_1) -$

$\quad\quad\quad T_2(F_0) \displaystyle\int_{-D_0}^{F_0} f(\tau_1) d(\tau_1) + (1 + b - h)\lambda_{41} = 0$

(21.5) $\quad \dfrac{\partial G_4}{\partial \lambda_{41}} = (1 + b - h)(F_0 + D_0) - \displaystyle\sum_{i=1}^{N} L_i = 0$

where W_i ($W_i \geqslant 0$) is the shadow price of the loan size constraint, i.e., it reflects the amount that the bank is willing to pay for a dollar increase in the loan to borrower i.

The necessary conditions for optimum are:

$$\dfrac{\partial G_4}{\partial L_i} = \dfrac{\partial G_4}{\partial F_0} \dfrac{1}{(1 + b - h)} = \dfrac{\partial G_4}{\partial L_j} \text{ for all } i, j.$$

Hence:

(22) $[V_i^*(1 + \eta V_i^* - W_i] = \dfrac{1}{(1+b-h)}[bT_1{}'(C) + T_2{}'(F_0)$

$$\int_{-D_0}^{F_0} (F_0 - \tau_1)f(\tau_1) + T_2(F_0)\int_{-D_0}^{F_0} f(\tau_1)d(\tau_1)$$

$= [V_j^*(1 + \eta V_j) - W_j]$ for all i,j $i \neq j$.

The optimality conditions (22) state that the marginal return to information minus the shadow price of the size constraint (W_i) should be the same for any two loans and equal to the marginal transaction costs of raising funds according to a fixed proportion determined by the leverage constraint.

The proportion of equity capital and borrowed funds in a bank's liabilities (the leverage constraint) and the share of riskless assets in the bank's portfolio (reserve requirements) are explicitly determined by the regulatory constraints. It is clear that for a given credit portfolio, the leverage constraint and reserve requirements reduce the probability of bank failures; however, these constraints also affect the credit portfolio selection. In order to examine the induced changes in the investment decision (credit portfolio selection), the optimality conditions of unregulated (equation 2B-5.2) and regulated (equation 21.1.2) banks are compared. Recall that equation 2B-5.2 states:

$$V_i(1 + \eta V_i) - \lambda_{31} + \lambda_{32}\left(\frac{\partial \mu_{P3}}{\partial L_i} + Z(\alpha)\frac{\partial \sigma_{P3}}{\partial L_i}\right) = 0 \quad i = 1, \ldots, N$$

The major difference between the optimality conditions of the two types of banks is that the expression that represents the impact of loans on the safety-first constraint of unregulated banks is omitted in the decision-making process of regulated banks.[22] Hence, regulated banks ignore the riskiness (i.e., rate of substitution between risk and return) of different loans and concentrate on returns from their portfolio. In other words, regulatory constraints on leverage size and reserve requirements lead banks to eliminate their concern about overall risk. Therefore, regulated banks tend to undertake riskier loans which, in an unregulated environment, they would have rejected, which has adverse effects on portfolio constraints. For example, consider a risky loan that increases the variance-risk of the bank and decreases its market value by more than the net returns from information it provides (i.e., $V_i(1 + \eta V_i) - \lambda_{31}$ in equation 2B-5.2), and hence is rejected ($\gamma_i > 0$). Such a loan would have been granted under the portfolio constraints imposed by regulation, and thus would have led to an increase in the risk of bank failure.

A comparison of the credit portfolio selection under current regulatory constraints to that under intended (direct chance constraint) regulation reveals a basic difference. Whereas the intended effect of regulatory constraints is to decrease the rate of substitution between risk and return in all decisions, including investments (credit portfolio), such constraints eliminate any risk considerations which are liable to increase the variance-risk of a loan portfolio.[23] Generally, under the assumed decision-making process of unregulated banks, the set of portfolio constraints should define and control all types of risk; if it did not, a bank might partially offset the regulatory efforts by increasing the risk of its unconstrained activities because of the elimination of the safety-first constraint.

It is important to note that portfolio constraints and bank examination processes restrict the risk of a bank's credit portfolio. Recall that three types of constraints are distinguished: 1) loan size constraints that limit the proportion of loans made to a single borrower in the bank's credit portfolio and force the bank to achieve some minimum diversification; 2) permissible activities constraints that prohibit bank expansion into other (potentially) risky activities;[24] and 3) bank examination processes that are used extensively for evaluating the riskiness of the credit portfolios. (The effectiveness of bank examiners will be discussed further in the following section.) Each of these measures puts an upper bound on the riskiness of banks' loan portfolios. The empirical question, however, is to what extent do they prevent any adverse effects with respect to the intended effect of capital adequacy regulation. Empirical evidence from the United States will be discussed in an attempt to answer this question following the analysis of the bank decision-making process under portfolio constraints and deposit insurance.

C. The Individual Bank's Decision-Making Process Under Deposit Insurance and Portfolio Constraints

In some countries capital adequacy regulation is affected through deposit insurance and portfolio constraints. Deposit insurance premiums for insured banks currently are charged at a constant rate on all deposits, whereas appropriate market compensations are increasing functions of a bank's overall variance-risk.[25] Banks have incentives to decrease their capital or to increase their asset risk, because the FDIC bears (buys) the additional default risk without appropriate compensation by the bank. Therefore, wealth-maximizing bank owners would tend to take higher risks than they would normally take if the FDIC were not insuring most of their deposits against losses to depositors.[26] Accordingly, bank stockholders follow an investment (loans granting) criterion that reflects potential wealth transfers from the FDIC that would result from changes in the bank's variance-risk.

Thus, the risk incentive effect counteracts the basic rationale for bank regulation, namely, monitoring the soundness of the banking system. Note that under portfolio constraints, adverse effects may result because banks are not concerned with the impact of loans on their overall risk; whereas, under deposit insurance, banks have *incentives* to increase the variance-risk of their loan portfolios.

Current deposit insurance plans eliminate the danger of losses for most depositors, as well as greatly reduce the probability of bank runs. Thus, at first glance, there no longer appears to be a need for portfolio constraints, as argued by Kreps and Wacht (1971). However, regulatory agencies still use portfolio constraints and heavy supervision, for two purposes. First, supervision and capital requirements are ways of protecting the FDIC's funds. The government (FDIC) is concerned, like any other lender, about the bank's overall riskiness; therefore, it constrains and examines banks to monitor the riskiness of their activities. A second reason for the use of portfolio constraints and supervision by regulatory agencies is the fact that, although deposit insurance decreases the potential danger of externalities, it does not completely eliminate them. These externalities still exist in uninsured banks and, to some extent, in insured banks because of uninsured large deposits. Thus, under the current system, solvency regulations are not a substitute for but a complement to deposit insurance.

Empirical evidence in the United States suggests that the FDIC has accumulated funds (profits) during the period of its existence (since 1935).[27] This observation suggests, in turn, that banks, on average, do not expropriate the FDIC.[28] The presence of regulation control over banks' decision-making— namely, portfolio constraints and bank examination—can explain the behavior of banks' stockholders. The ways in which portfolio constraints and bank examination prevent banks from expropriating the FDIC are discussed next.

1. Portfolio Constraints

The effect of changes in the variance-risk upon the value of stockholders' claims implies that banks do not necessarily accept only those loans with positive net returns from information; some loans that increase the market value of the stockholders' claims by increasing the variance-risk also would be accepted. It is argued that portfolio constraints are likely to reduce investment incentives for the following reasons. First, the leverage constraint reduces the potential increase in the market value of stockholders' claims from a given increase in the variance-risk. Second, the loan "size" and the "permissible" activities constraints determine (reduce) the available investment opportunity set of banks and hence, the level of riskiness that can be achieved through the investment decision. Consequently, bank stockholders' abilities to pursue their investment incentive policies are constrained by portfolio restrictions.[29] Evidently, deposit insurance premiums are set at levels which, when combined with the portfolio constraints, prevent the possibility that banks in the aggregate will expropriate FDIC's claims.

2. Bank Examination

The bank examination process also is utilized to protect the FDIC's funds against excessive risk taking by individual banks. Credit portfolio selection is the major decision not controlled by portfolio constraints; therefore, regulators use a bank's examination process extensively for evaluating credit portfolios. As pointed out by Benston (1973):

> . . . the largest part of the examination is devoted to an evaluation of the credit-worthiness of the bank's loans. The percentages vary from bank to bank and among supervisory agencies, but it is generally agreed that one half or more of the examiners' time is devoted to loans and collateral. . . . (P. 8)

Orgler (1968) indicates that "over two thirds of the time spent by the FDIC examiners is devoted to loan evaluations" (p. 11). Thus, it is important to examine the effectiveness of bank examiners in analyzing and pointing out potentially bad loans and problem banks.

Wu (1969) studies examiners' criticisms and subsequent loan defaults in a random sample of 33 national banks and concludes that "our study, though not definitive, suggests that bank examiners' criticisms of business loans are reasonably accurate. . ." (p. 705). But his conclusion must be tempered by the small size of the sample and lack of supportive evidence. Benston (1973) examines the effectiveness of bank examiners in classifying problem banks and finds that:

> . . . the examiners' ability in spotting banks that are likely to fail is far from perfect, . . . Of the 56 banks that failed from January 1959 through April 1971 only 41 percent were classified as problems at the time of the examination approximately one year before failure. Of these, a little more than half were rated serious problem banks. And of the 59 percent not rated as problems, a little more than half were given the highest rating. (P. 43)

Sinky (1978) uses discriminant analysis to reclassify examiner determined categories of problem banks. His sample includes 143 commercial banks from the FDIC's March 31, 1974 problem bank list, and a random sample of 163 non-problem banks. He concludes:

> On average, substandard loans account for about 80 percent of a problem bank's classified loans. Finally, banks that failed in recent years almost invariably had large volumes of substandard loans (relative to their capital and reserves) sixteen to twenty-two months before failure: however, most banks with low [NCR's] do not fail. (P. 191)

Thus, although there is no supportive evidence for the effectiveness of bank examination alone in limiting bank risk, the combined effect of bank examination *and* portfolio constraint does tend to limit bank's investment incentives and to restrain them from expropriating FDIC's claims. These findings do not rule out the possibility of adverse effects from bank regulation, because if the deposit premium is set high enough, banks could increase their riskiness without expropriating FDIC's claims.[30] Evidently, Peltzman (1970) and Mingo (1975) found that banks increased their riskiness following the establishment of the deposit insurance.

In conclusion, the effectiveness of capital adequacy regulation in those countries that use portfolio constraints depends on the magnitude of the adverse effects on the unconstrained decisions. In countries that use deposit insurance and portfolio constraints, the danger of loss for most depositors is eliminated and also the probability of bank runs is substantially reduced. The United States experience suggests that portfolio constraints are effective, on average, in reducing stockholders' investment incentives. But consideration of the efficiency and social costs also are required to evaluate different sets of bank regulations. These costs are discussed in the following section.

III.3   Social and Private Costs of the Regulatory Process

Two major types of costs of bank regulation may be distinguished. One is the cost of foregone opportunities to the public and the banks to the extent that bank regulation inhibits the efficient allocation of resources. In particular, under current regulations in the United States, a fixed insurance premium is charged and an attempt is made to restrict a bank's probability of bankruptcy. The combined effect of these two factors is likely to constrain the bank's decision-making process. The decrease in a bank's market value can be analyzed by comparing the decision-making process of regulated versus unregulated banks within the framework of the model developed in this study. This expected reduction represents, to some extent, a misallocation of resources (social costs) in the economy. The second cost of bank regulation includes the explicit costs of maintaining the regulatory function, and the implicit costs of any inefficiencies inherent in this process.

A. The Effect of Capital Adequacy Regulation on the Bank's Market Value[31]

The impact of reserve requirements is ignored in this analysis since it is considered part of the costs of the monetary system. The analysis first considers the impact of regulatory constraints on the feasible set of investment opportunities a bank faces and on the transaction costs associated with issuing claims. Then the impacts of changes in the bank's investment and financing decisions on the expected costs of bankruptcy (safety-first constraint) are analyzed.

1. The Distortion of the Financing Decision

Regulatory constraints require a bank to issue financial claims in a certain (fixed) composition that does not necessarily coincide with the one determined in the unregulated maximization process. Within the framework of the unregulated bank's decision-making process discussed in Chapter III, such a non-optimal financial structure could affect the bank's market value by imposing larger transaction costs for issuing claims. Transaction costs that the bank bears by reducing its debt-equity ratio include flotation, conflict of interest, and the cost of taxes.[32] Generally, these transaction costs are assumed to be relatively low and, in fact, similar constraints frequently are used for contracts in the private lending market. Also, among the countries surveyed in this study, the most restrictive leverage constraint requires banks' equity capital to amount to at least 15 percent of its total liabilities. The average requirement (across countries) requires banks to have equity capital that amounts to at least 8 percent of total assets. Thus, the magnitude of the induced change by the regulatory constraint in the composition of a bank's financial claims cannot be large. Therefore, the reduction in a bank's market value resulting from the distortion in the financing decision is assumed to be relatively low.

2. The Distortion in the Investment Decision

The regulatory process in general, and the constraints on the investment decision in particular, affect a bank's returns to information and, hence, the market value of the bank. The major part of a regulation's impact on the investment decision stems from its indirect effects on the bank-customer relationship. These effects are implicit in the model of a bank's decision-making process under regulatory constraints discussed in Section III.2.

The ceiling on the amount of a loan to any single borrower and the permissible activities constraint restrict the investment opportunity set of banks. A restriction on the amount loaned to any single borrower may force a bank to assume only part of some loans (i.e., joining with other banks to provide such loans).[33] This joint venture with other banks imposes additional costs that decrease returns accrued in providing loans. Furthermore, as pointed out earlier in Section II.2, banking with a number of banks reduces the return to information (V_i), i.e., the relative advantage of cost-free access to information about customers is reduced. Therefore, the size of the loan constraint reduces a bank's return from lending and also prevents the bank from exploiting all of its return opportunities, thereby leading to a decrease in the bank's market value.

The permissible activities constraint prevents any affiliation between the bank and the customer corporation that increases the cost of information to the bank, and in turn, reduces the return to information from lending. Also, the almost cost-free information about customers gained through the provision of banking services allows a bank additional returns to information in related financial services markets such as mortgage loans, underwriting, insurance, and the issuance of credit cards. It can be argued that, under conditions of uncertainty concerning customers' activities and performances, there are economies of scale to be gained from producing a diversified mix of financial services. Therefore, regulatory constraints that restrict a bank's access to some relevant financial sources markets impose production inefficiencies and, hence, reduce a bank's market value.

3. Probability of Bank Failure

Changes in the bank's financing and investment decisions affect the probability of bank failure and hence, also the bank's market value. If regulation is successful in decreasing the probability of bank failure and consequently the expected cost of bankruptcy, a bank's market value will increase and partially offset distortions in the bank decision-making process. In addition, the permissible activity constraint decreases the marginal cost of reducing the probability of bankruptcy. Heggestad (1975) found that the returns to some closely related nonbank activities were negatively correlated with those of commercial banks; thus, the permissible activity constraint, and to some extent the size-of-loan constraint, increases the marginal cost of reducing the probability of bankruptcy.

B. Pareto Optimality Considerations

The impact of the regulatory process on the bank's market value represents, to some extent, a redistribution of wealth among banks and in the economy as a whole and also a misallocation of resources in the economy (social cost).

The constraint on the financing decision represents a social cost to the extent that it forces a bank to operate with a nonoptimal composition of sources, which leads to higher transaction costs. The flotation and agency (conflict of interest) costs are real costs to the bank as well as to the economy since they result in the consumption of real resources. On the other hand, the tax effect on a bank's market value *per se* represents only a redistribution of wealth within the economy.

Constraints on the investment decision may result in a misallocation of resources to the extent that the cost of the production of banking and financial services in other sectors of the economy will be higher, particularly the cost of information. Constraints may also prevent banks from supplying financial services which, because of the information they possess, can produce at lower costs than can other segments in the economy. In addition, the size-of-loan constraint increases the real social costs of information due to the participation of other banks in the provision of large loans. The effect of the investment incentive upon the value of stockholders' claims is that the banks do not necessarily accept all loans with non-negative net returns, nor do they reflect all loans with negative net returns. Change in the variance-risk reflects a wealth transfer from the bank's claimholders (including the FDIC) to its stockholders that might be accomplished by undertaking loans with negative returns or rejecting loans with positive net returns. The granting of loans with negative market values and rejection of loans with positive market values because of the investment incentive reduces the social welfare.[34]

Finally, cost-benefit considerations of capital adequacy regulations require that the social costs imposed by regulatory constraints should be equal to the social benefits. However, the portfolio constraints imposed by regulators and the fixed insurance premium charged all banks regardless of their production function is unlikely to result in a social optimum. The social optimum condition states that the expected marginal (social) costs of bankruptcy should be equal to the distortions in the investment and financing decisions resulting from a decrease in the probability of bankruptcy. Therefore, regulatory constraints that do not consider a bank's production function are not likely to preserve the optimality condition.

In conclusion, regulatory constraints on the bank's investment and financing decisions induce a misallocation of resources (real costs), which is a major consideration in cost-benefit analysis of bank regulation. Other determinants of the social costs of bank regulation are the costs of the regulatory function. These costs are analyzed in the following section.

C. The Costs of the Regulatory Function

The costs of the regulatory process include the "direct" costs of maintaining the regulatory function and costs incurred as a result of inefficient bank regulation. The inefficiencies of bank regulation result from possible conflicts of interest that arise from administration by imperfect agents who maximize their welfare rather than serve the public's interest, and also from inefficiencies in the portfolio regulations.

1. Direct Costs of the Regulatory Function

The direct costs of maintaining the regulatory function—examining and supervising the banking industry—are important social costs associated with the regulatory process. Benston (1973, p. 55) provides some measurements of these costs over time and of the number of personnel working in examination and supervisory capacities. In addition, substantial direct costs are imposed on banks by the regulation, e.g., disrupted work schedules, preparation of documents, etc. Furthermore, regulators are constantly changing their requirements, e.g., they may change their capital standard on very short notice, thereby imposing additional costs of regulation on banks. These costs are considerable, particularly when compared to the total loss from failed banks.[35]

2. Agency Costs of Bank Regulation

Thus far the regulator has been viewed as an absolutely loyal agent who operates in the public interest, i.e., maximizing social welfare. The agency officials' pronouncements clearly declare that they are acting as loyal agents and in the public's best interests. For example, the Federal Reserve System's ex-chairman Arthur Burns (1974) says,

> In the past year, we have had the largest bank failures in the nation's history. This fact has been widely noticed, as it deserves to be. But, it is equally important to recognize that these failures did not cause *any loss to depositors.* Nor did they have *serious repercussions on other banks or businesses.* The ability of our financial system to absorb such shocks *reflects credit on the safeguards that Congress has* developed in response to past experiences. (Pp. 1-2, emphasis added)

However, it should be recognized that the use of any agent raises the possibility of conflicts of interest. In seeking to maximize his wealth by ensuring his tenure in office, a regulator is unlikely to maximize the social welfare. Suppose that a regulator believes his tenure in office depends, in part, on his capability to prevent bank failures.[36] Given this political environment, he has an incentive to minimize the probability of bank failures. Further, as Black, *et. al.,* (1978) point out, some bank regulations reveal the agencies' tendencies toward regulatory expansion, which imposes costs on the depositors.

The regulators' desire of welfare maximization is likely to lead them to be reluctant to close a bank even when it is in the best interest of the public, thereby increasing the social costs imposed by bank regulations.[37] Some support for this argument can be found in past FDIC behavior as indicated by Barnett, *et. al.,* (1977) who state:

> In 1951, a congressional committee was severely critical of what seemed to be an automatic FDIC decision to use the purchase and assumption alternative in all bank failures. In fact, there had been no payoffs between 1944 and 1951, and comparative cost tests had been virtually ignored. The result, of course, could be predicted; one bank with total assets of only $637 thousand required an outlay by the FDIC of $1.8 million, to effect FDIC assisted purchase and assumption with accompanying indemnities to the takover bank. (Pp. 314-15)

3. The Inefficiency of Portfolio Constraints

Portfolio constraints deal separately with each type of risk and do not allow any substitution among different types of risk within the general constraint of the probability of bankruptcy. If regulators could impose a direct constraint on the probability of bank failure, banks, as rational wealth-maximizing economic agents, would follow the alternative which minimizes the reduction in their market value. Clearly, the optimal policy differs in various banks depending on their investment opportunity set and on the interaction between investment and financing decisions. Therefore, rigid portfolio requirements impose additional constraints on the substitution of risk which stems from different decisions and, hence, additional social costs.

In summary, portfolio requirements are inefficient since they do not consider the differences in costs resulting from the constraints on each bank's decision making. Banks also are prohibited from any substitution among different types of risk. Hence, portfolio constraints lead to a larger reduction in banks' market values than could have been caused by the direct chance constraint. As is concluded earlier, systems that include both deposit insurance and portfolio constraints are effective; however, they suffer from the deficiencies of the portfolio constraints and, in addition, from the investment incentive (constrained by capital adequacy regulations) and regulators' agency costs. These deficiencies call for reconsideration of and suggestions for improvement in the existing regulatory system.

III.4   Improving the Regulatory Process

Recommendations for improvement in the existing regulatory systems derived from this analysis are A) elimination of portfolio constraints, B) assessment of banks' riskiness through the capital market, and C) adoption of risk-related deposit insurance rates.

A. Elimination of Portfolio Constraints

It can be concluded from the discussion in this chapter that constraints that can limit the probability of bankruptcy are very difficult (effectiveness) and expensive (efficiency) to implement. Therefore, it follows that regulators should use their monopoly power and intervene only when necessary. Black, *et. al.,* (1978) point out the similarity between the portfolio constraints regulators impose on banks and the requirements a lender imposes on a borrower in the private market. But there is one important and significant difference. In the private market, lenders protect themselves by an agreement that specifies the risk they bear and the appropriate compensation for this risk. Lenders have no way to take any action to protect themselves beyond the legal contract (agreement); therefore, such an agreement between borrowers and lenders is very important in the private lending market. The government, however, has the legal and economic power to intervene whenever it feels necessary. Therefore, it should limit its activities to imposing constraints on banks that violate the general constraint on the probability of bankruptcy. Santomero and Vinso's (1977) findings that only a small number of banks exhibit high risk support this proposal.

This proposed regulatory scheme eliminates most of the deficiencies of the existing systems. It rules out any adverse effect from a bank's behavior since the overall variance-risk is measured and controlled. Furthermore, regulators would be able to intervene and impose constraints (penalties) on various banks at different levels of riskiness; i.e., according to the social cost-benefit of the additional risk undertaken by each bank.[38] Finally, banks would be allowed to pursue their optimal policies to meet regulators' requirements.

The effectiveness and the practical significance of this proposal depends on the existence of an efficient (accurate) measure of a bank's overall risk. This is an important issue since the efficiency of bank examiners in predicting bank failures in advance has been questioned in several studies (discussed and cited earlier). The following section suggests that capital market data might be used to construct such measures.

B. Assessment of Banks' Risk through the Capital Market

Many empirical studies have found that the capital market is "efficient" in the sense that asset prices behavior continuously "reflects" all available information (see Fama, 1976, for a review). Accordingly, one should be able to estimate banks' overall variance-risk using stock price data, at least as successfully as by using accounting data.

The advantages of using stock market data for bank regulation include: (a) the market provides an estimate of a bank's overall variance-risk that simultaneously incorporates changes in different types of risk; (b) the regulatory costs of implementing such measures are not significant since data are readily available; (c) the market prices of stocks "correct" for misleading book value measures used by bank examiners; (d) the use of stock market data (particularly daily prices) provides regulators with an instantaneous measure of changes in a bank's overall variance-risk and allows them to make an immediate response. In terms of the model of a regulated bank discussed earlier, stock prices provide a direct measure of the actual effect of regulation (as opposed to the intended effect).

It is important to note that the number of U.S. banks that issue securities traded in organized capital markets is a small portion of the banking industry (several hundred out of about 14,000 banks). However, assuming that total assets is the variable (proxy) responsible for differences in the costs to the agencies of bank regulation, a major part of regulatory costs are due to this group.[39] Thus, to the extent that security prices serve as an alternative source of data, they could affect a major part of regulatory costs. Furthermore, the number of banks that issue securities traded in organized stock markets has grown rapidly in recent years, especially bank holding companies; therefore, reliance on this source of data for regulatory purposes could be extended in the future.

Finally, an attempt to predict corporate failure was made by Beaver (1968) and Altman (1968) who found that stock prices indeed predicted failure sooner than did individual financial ratios. In Chapter V of this study, a measure of bank variance-risk is suggested and used to estimate changes in banks' overall variance-risk over time.[40] Further, tests of the effects of regulation of bank holding companies on the variance-risk and profitability of affected banks are conducted.

C. Risk-Related Insurance Rates

Risk-related insurance rates have been proposed and considered at length.[41] The variable rate premium conceivably provides a substitute for the market discipline that is reduced by the insurance system. Under this system, each bank would be free to choose its risk according to a schedule of risk premiums. A clear advantage of this scheme is that it prevents the risk incentive deficiency discussed earlier, and it also allows individual banks to make unconstrained portfolio decisions.[42] However, objections have been raised to this premium system. First, it seems that, at present, regulators exaggerate the degree of externalities, probably as a result of the agent conflict discussed earlier. The possibility that regulators are reluctant to close a bank may lead them to reject the variable insurance premiums scheme. It is not probable that a regulator would allow a bank to choose its level of risk as long as the appropriate insurance premium is met, because increased risk of bank failure decreases the regulator's welfare.

The second argument is that a risk premium system is very costly to administer because of the dynamic nature of bank decision-making. For example, liabilities and investments in banking are subject to almost instantaneous changes. The very short horizon of decision-making in banking relative to other industries makes the suggested rate mechanism very costly to administer. Third, it is extremely difficult to assess risk of failure on an actuarial basis, as noted by Barnett, et. al., (1977). However, this problem exists as well under the present system of capital adequacy regulation. Furthermore, to some extent, similar problems exist in any insurance plan in other areas. Nevertheless, the FDIC has never considered the implementation of a variable insurance premium, despite frequent suggestions for changes and the possible advantages.

Finally, it is important to recognize the dynamic nature of the regulatory process. Although most U.S. bank failures in the past (1940-1971) have involved very small banks, recent failures have involved progressively larger banks. Until 1971, the largest U.S. bank to fail had total deposits of $93 million, whereas Franklin National Bank of New York, which failed in 1974, had total deposits of $1.4 billion (see Horvitz, 1975, Table 1). The increased insolvency on the part of the banking system in general, and large banks in particular, is to some extent a result of the changing nature and structure of bank activities. The most important changes are the development of the bank holding company form of organization, and the use of practices such as liability management and foreign operations. If this were the case, appropriate adjustments in the regulatory process would be required.

The following chapter examines the rationale for the development of the bank holding company form of organization in the U.S. banking industry. Banks' rationale for forming bank holding companies, particularly their expansion into nonbank activities, and bank regulators' (and legislative) attitudes toward this phenomenon are analyzed. The normative models of banks' decision-making processes (Chapter II) and bank regulation behavior (Chapter III) provide a useful framework for such analysis. In addition, the number of banks that issue equity capital traded in capital markets has been growing rapidly in recent years.[43] This fact provides an opportunity to use the proposed method of bank regulation, namely the use of stock prices, for the regulatory process. In Chapter V tests (measures) are made of the actual effects of both expansion into nonbank activities and of the regulation of bank holding companies on the variance-risk and profitability of affected banks.

Chapter IV

The Development and Regulation
of Bank Holding Companies

The bank holding company (BHC) form of organization appears to dominate the U.S. banking industry. By 1977, bank holding companies controlled almost 4,000 banks that held 69 percent of all bank deposits. First, this chapter provides a brief history of development and regulation of bank holding companies since the Bank Holding Company Act of 1956. Then the rationale for nonbank expansion of BHCs is analyzed using the normative model of an individual bank's decision-making process presented in Chapters II and III. Finally, different aspects of BHC regulation are examined using the model of bank regulation discussed in Chapter III.

IV.1 Background and Historical Perspective

The movement in recent years in the United States of banks forming holding companies has been rapid and has had a significant impact on both the financial services industry and its consumers. Several of the constraints imposed on banks have been partially alleviated by this structural change. This is particularly true for the forced separation of banks from various other segments of the financial services industry and from the geographical limitations on branching both within and among states. Nevertheless, the formation of bank holding companies and their operations are subject to approval by regulatory authorities.

The BHC Act of 1956 was the first legislation aimed at the group banking movement. This Act defined the *multibank* holding company, required each such company to register with the Federal Reserve Board, and specified that the Board approve bank acquisitions, mergers, and the formation of new BHCs. The act prohibits interstate banking and resulted in a distinct dichotomy between the operations of a one-bank holding company and nonbank activities.

Despite the Federal Reserve's and the Comptroller of Currency's recommendation of the one-bank definition of a BHC (i.e., a company that controls at least 25 percent of one bank), the 1956 Act specified a two-bank (multibank) definition. Thus, the act granted a blanket exclusion to companies owning only one bank. In most cases, one-bank holding companies were established by issuing shares of the BHC in exchange for a bank's shares and the bank's shares became the only asset of the new BHC. Later the bank remained the dominant organization within the holding company, which then expanded into nonbank fields. In fact, one-bank holding companies have expanded primarily into closely related nonbank financial fields, and also into various industrial fields such as metal mining and petroleum refining, etc. (see *Federal Reserve Bulletin,* December 1972, page A99 for a detailed list). The regulatory status of a one-bank holding company before 1970 can be characterized as follows: they were not required to register with the Federal Reserve, and hence their nonbank expansion was not regulated (constrained). In order to retain their non-regulated status, however, one-bank holding companies were prohibited from acquiring banks. The Federal Reserve continuously pressured for inclusion of a provision for regulating one-bank groups. However, it was not until the 1970 Amendment that it succeeded. Under these circumstances, it is not surprising that the growth of registered (multibank) holding companies was moderate. The number of registered holding companies rose from 53 in 1956 to 123 in 1970 and their share of total deposits grew from 8.3 percent in 1956 to 16.2 percent in 1970 (source: *Federal Reserve Bulletins*).

The 1970 Amendment to the BHC Act broadened the definition of a BHC to include one-bank holding companies. Consequently, the number of registered bank holding companies increased from 121 at the end of 1970 to 1,567 at the end of 1971 and their total deposits as a percentage of all bank deposits increased from 16.2 percent in 1970 to 55.1 in 1971. The 1970 Amendment also permitted the former one-bank groups to acquire or establish new banks as affiliates, as well as to continue to expand into permissible nonbank activities. Indeed, the law required the Federal Reserve Board to establish standards for determining the nonbank activities into which BHCs would be permitted to expand. In deciding whether to permit a BHC to engage in a particular activity, the Board determines whether the activity is closely related to banking, and whether the performance of the activity by the proposed affiliate is expected to produce benefits to the public that outweigh possible adverse effects [Section 4(c)(8) of the amendment]. Categories ruled on by the Board of Governors as of the end of 1977 are listed in Table 4-1.

The legislative process of the nonbank expansion provision has spawned a long debate among legislators about potential social costs and benefits of these provisions.[1] Evidently, the 1970 legislation did not end this controversy, but rather affected the way in which the Board administered the act.

During the 1970-1974 period, expansion of BHCs into both bank and nonbank activities was significant. The Board's positive attitude toward this expansion is evidenced by the short processing time of each application and the

Table 4-1

Activities Permitted as "Closely Related to Banking" as of December 10, 1977

Permitted by regulation
1. Extensions of credit
    a. Mortgage banking
    b. Finance companies: consumer, sales, and commercial
    c. Credit cards
    d. Factoring
2. Industrial bank, industrial loan company
3. Servicing loans
4. Trust company
5. Investment or financial advisory
6. Leasing of personal and real property
7. Investments in community welfare projects
8. Providing bookkeeping or data processing services
9. Acting as insurance agent or broker—primarily in connection with credit extensions
10. Underwriting credit life and credit accident, and health insurance
11. Issuance and sale of travelers checks
12. Buying and selling gold and silver bullion and silver coin
13. Providing courier services
14. Management consulting for unaffiliated banks
15. Issuing money orders
16. Future commission merchant to execute futures contracts covering gold and silver bullion and coins.

Activities Prohibited by the Board
1. Insurance premium funding
2. Underwriting life insurance not related to credit extension
3. Real estate brokerage
4. Land development
5. Real estate syndication
6. Management consulting
7. Property management
8. Computer output microfilm services
9. Underwriting mortgage guaranty insurance
10. Operating a savings and loan association
11. Operating a travel agency

Activities Under Consideration
1. Underwriting and dealing in obligations of the United States and certain municipal securities

_____

Source: "Bank Expansion Quarterly," Vol. XXI, December 1977, Carter Golembe Assoc. Inc., Washington, D.C.

high percentage of approvals (93 percent of all applications).[2] In mid-1974, however, the Federal Reserve became concerned that the activities of BHCs and their nonbank affiliates would increase the risk of bank failure and of losses to depositors and the FDIC. Therefore, the Federal Reserve Board adopted a so-called "go-slow" policy that extended the processing period of applications, increased the rate of denial orders, and did not approve any additional nonbank activities. This "go-slow" policy reflects the existing confusion about the social costs and benefits resulting from the nonbank expansion of BHCs.[3] Moreover the nonbank expansion of BHCs raised a related issue as to the appropriate degree of regulation of these organizations, i.e., whether to engage in detailed examination and regulation of all holding companies, or to leave such supervision to market forces.

IV.2 The Rationale for Nonbank Expansion of BHCs

The rationale for nonbank expansion by BHCs is analyzed within the decision-making process of regulated banks discussed in Chapter III under specific assumptions regarding the BHCs' behavior.[4] BHCs are assumed to be market value maximizers operating in an uncertain environment, and they and their subsidiaries are further assumed to form a synergistic merger, in the sense that their operational decisions are dependent.[5] This synergy assumption suggests that a BHC and its subsidiaries operate as a unified entity where each subsidiary acts in coordination with all other subsidiaries to maximize a single objective function for the entire organization. This assumption implies that investment and financing decisions are made by taking into consideration their joint impact on all subsidiaries.

There are, however, two possible constraints on the behavior of BHCs as a synergistic merger. First, there are possible conflicts of interest among different groups of stockholders. Such conflicts may arise if market value maximization of a subsidiary involves policies different from those for the market value-maximization of the BHC. In fact, almost all nonbank subsidiaries are fully controlled (100 percent of shares) by the BHC, presumably to obviate such conflicts of interest. In cases where a conflict of interest does exist, it is assumed that a costless compensation scheme exists (i.e., a redistribution of wealth among groups of stockholders) that allows the subsidiary to follow the policy that maximizes the market value of the parent BHC. A second constraint limits the amount of investment (outflow of funds) by a bank subsidiary in other affiliates of the BHC.

The effects of BHC expansion into nonbank activities on investment and financing decisions, and the risk of failure of the BHC and affiliated banks, are analyzed in the following section under the synergy assumption of the BHC.

A. The Investment Rationale

The expansion of BHCs into nonbank activities is expected to provide banks with a comparative advantage in producing closely related financial services (e.g., credit card systems, mortgage banking, and trust companies). In these services, as well as in banking activities, information serves as a major factor of production. Therefore, a bank's advantage in acquiring and analyzing information about customers financial conditions provides it with added returns to information from producing these complementary services as discussed in Section II.2. This is particularly true for those BHC customers who already have been purchasing banking services and about whom information is readily available. It is argued that expected production efficiency is the reason that the 1970 Amendment to the BHC Act required that activities of nonbank subsidiaries of BHCs will be functionally related to banking, where "functionally" implies joint production and purchase using the same input, particularly information. This joint production may increase the returns from information and/or reduce the market price of financial services. It is clear that the financial services, production decisions, and acquisition of information depend on their impact on the parent BHCs. A related rationale for the nonbank expansion of BHCs is the convenience customers gain from purchasing financial services from a single institution; this leads to production and consumption efficiency.

B. The Financing Rationale

BHCs' parent companies attain economies of scale by issuing financial claims to perform the financial function of the entire group. They provide operating funds to their existing affiliates that affect their leverage position. The evidence cited by Talley (1975), and Heggestad-Mingo (1975) indicates that the ratio of equity capital to total assets for large BHCs appears to be significantly lower than that of independent banks. Furthermore, the capital-to-asset ratios of banks acquired by BHCs tend to decline subsequent to their affiliation.[6] Also the group enjoys the advantage of possibly shifting resources among subsidiaries according to their investment opportunities, at transaction costs lower than those borne when issuing external claims; the flow of funds within the group, however, is limited by law. The subsidiary bank may lend up to 10 percent of its capital to any one affiliate and up to 20 percent of its capital to all affiliates. It also can transfer funds through dividends to the parent firm or management fees to other affiliates. The extent to which these methods can be used is limited, and transaction costs may be involved (e.g., taxes on dividends).

To summarize, a BHC gains production efficiency through the combined effect of financing and investment decisions; also, nonbank activities provide the BHC with diversification opportunities.

C. The Risk of Bank Failure

As affiliates of a BHC, banks are maintained as legally separated corporate entities that are isolated from any financial difficulties arising in other subsidiaries. Legally a subsidiary of a holding company generally is not liable for debts of any other subsidiary of the holding company. The only consequence of a subsidiary failure that leads to failure of a BHC is a transfer of bank ownership. Several authors argue that this legal separation may give the false impression that banks are insulated from problems in other subsidiaries;[7] this is not true because of the externality effect on bank creditors' behavior. The public may equate BHCs' problems with those of their nonbank affiliates even though the holding companies are reasonably sound. There is evidence to support this contention. Orgler and Wolkowitz (1976, p. 78) cite the Beverly Hills Bancorp failure, and Silverberg (1975, p. 204) uses the Southern California bank experience as an example. Mayne (1978, p. 731) cites several additional cases where bank failures were related to loss of the nonbank affiliates of the respective holding companies. In addition, Black, *et. al.* (1978, p. 395) provide possible legal justification for unlimited liability in a suit against the bank by an unsophisticated creditor of a nonbank subsidiary. Therefore, nonbank expansion may increase the likelihood of bank failure.

The expansion of BHCs into nonbank activities reduces the expected costs of bankruptcy (under the dependency hypothesis) for BHCs, e.g., by permitting greater service and geographical diversification. Heggestad (1975) has found that some currently permissible nonbank activities do exhibit returns that are negatively correlated with those in banking. Moreover, geographical diversification is attained by BHCs, since nonbank subsidiaries are not bound by state laws on branch banking. However, the gains from BHC diversification do not seem to be significant because of the small portion of holding companies' funds invested in nonbank activities, and the constraint that such activities must be closely related to banking.

To summarize, BHC expansion into nonbank activities affects the likelihood of the affiliated banks' failures; however, the direction of this effect is undetermined and is a fundamental issue in the regulation of BHCs.

IV.3 Capital Adequacy and the Regulation of BHCs

Banking supervision and regulation in the United States is aimed largely at protecting the FDIC's funds and preventing bank failures. Whatever the merits of that view, the Federal Reserve must consider any significant increase in the risk of bank failure that might arise from holding company affiliation. Currently, even though they have the authority to do so, regulators are not directly regulating BHC nonbank activities, and seldom have even examined them. One reason may be that any examination of BHCs would involve a substantial increase in the "direct" costs of the regulatory process. But does affiliation with a BHC lead to greater variance-risk for an affiliated bank than for banks that remain independent? To answer this question, one must identify specific risk mechanisms and their implications for the regulatory process. This is discussed next.

A. Direct Increase in the Risk of Bank Failures

Changes in the production of banking services, i.e., financing and investment policies of affiliated banks, may affect the risk of bank failure. The direction (as discussed earlier in Chapter II) of such a shift is not known *a priori* and is determined by changes in the riskiness of the loan portfolio and by possible changes in financial leverage. The implications of such shifts in risk are the same as those for any other changes in risk arising from the bank decision-making process. Therefore, a direct change in the risks of bank failure raises no additional dimensions and should be controlled adequately by capital adequacy regulation.

B. Indirect Increase in the Risk of Bank Failure

BHCs' subsidiaries often are closely associated with their parent companies and nonbank affiliates. This raises the possibility that a failure of the BHC as a result of losses in its nonbank activities may cause loss of confidence in the bank which could lead to a bank run. Such a run is possible either because depositors doubt the effectiveness of the regulatory process of the banking subsidiary or they regard troubles in the holding company as an indication of possible dishonesty and mismanagement of affiliated banks. In addition, the BHC might use its control over the bank to cover losses in the nonbank subsidiary even though such assistance might increase the risk of bank failure.[8] There are two principal ways a holding company could encounter serious financial difficulties (aside from banking subsidiaries): through its leverage position and through losses from its nonbank activities.[9]

The implications of this hypothesis for the regulation of BHCs are that one of three alternative procedures could be employed. (i) The regulators may attempt to remove any impression on the part of creditors of the nonbank subsidiary that they are dealing with the bank or that the bank was guaranteeing the debts of the nonbank affiliate (e.g., by using different names and locations as suggested by Black, *et. al.,* 1978). However, it seems clear that this operational separation is very costly and contradicts the basic element of joint production of financial services. Obviously, it is in the interest of the BHC to notify its customers of the production dependency among its bank and nonbank subsidiaries. As long as the dependency in production among subsidiaries exists it is expected that the creditors and the market will view management's problem in managing a nonbank subsidiary as information about the ability of the bank's management. (ii) The Board may consider excluding risky activities (relative to banking) from the list of permitted nonbank activities, or regulating the extent of BHCs' investments in nonbank activities. The expected social benefit of such restrictions should be compared with losses of efficiency in producing these services. (iii) Finally, the Board can choose to supervise the nonbank subsidiaries of BHCs. At the present time, nonbank activities represent a very small share of BHCs' assets (see Holland, 1975), and the potential added risks of those dimensions are not likely to constitute a threat of any major consequence to the banking industry as a whole. However, nonbank investment may and actually did affect the probability of an individual bank failure. Therefore, capital adequacy considerations should be based on evaluation of the entire organization. In particular, BHCs' leverage position is quite important since the financial position of the affiliated banks does not necessarily coincide with that of the BHC because of the double leverage practices. This phenomenon takes place when a bank holding company borrows money (debt) and invests it in equity securities in its key bank affiliates as discussed earlier.[10]

C. The Investment Incentive

As presented earlier in Chapter III, deposit insurance gives banks incentives to increase their risk and hence their market value, by expropriating the FDIC's claim. Nonbank activities expand the bank's investments opportunity set, thereby increasing bank stockholders' investment incentives (opportunities). The BHC may gain an advantage by draining the resources of the bank to support the other subsidiaries, or it might require the bank to undertake excessive risks in order to benefit another subsidiary. A BHC would only engage in such practices if the increase in the market value of the other subsidiaries is greater than its expected loss in the bank. The primary losers in such situations would be the depositors and the FDIC. Two examples of policies that increase the level of risk in bank portfolios are the acquisition of unsound assets from affiliates, and payment of high-dividend or management (services) fees to the parent BHC.[11] Nevertheless, it is important to note that the incentive to expropriate the FDIC's claim by increasing the bank's variance-risk is independent of the form of organization. The BHC form is relevant only if it enables banks to increase their risk and misleads regulators beyond the opportunities available to independent banks. But there is little reason to believe that transactions with affiliated firms are likely to mislead regulations, since they readily attract the examiners' attention.

A related hypothesis follows directly from the intersubsidiaries' dependency (externality) assumption that affiliated firms' failures indirectly affect the probability of a bank's failure. The BHCs can thwart regulators' goals to preserve the banking industry soundness by undertaking risky nonbank activities (subsidiaries) with expectations that regulators will protect them from financial failure in order to prevent customer loss of confidence in subsidiary banks. Nonbank subsidiary market value will increase as the cost of issuing debt decreases; i.e., because the expected regulatory protection may lead a nonbank subsidiary to undertake excessive risk without securing appropriate market compensation. The BHC organization serves also as a vehicle whereby bank subsidiaries can assume greater risk. Any increase in risk borne by nonbank subsidiaries increases the variance-risk and, consequently, the market value of bank shares.

One implication of this hypothesis to the regulation of BHCs is that the dependency between affiliated banks and nonbank subsidiaries would be eliminated with the expected consequences which were discussed earlier. Alternatively, the Federal Reserve Board might consider supervising the nonbank subsidiaries of BHCs so that the capital adequacy requirement can be adjusted according to the degree of risk. The investment incentive hypothesis and potential increase in risk for BHCs will lead to intervention by regulators regardless of the degree of nonbank activities in the BHC assets.

IV.4 Cost-Benefit Considerations of BHC Expansion into Nonbank Activities

The 1970 Amendment to the BHC Act and the Federal Reserve Board's initial administration of the law emphasized the expected benefits from this amendment. BHC expansion into nonbank activities was expected to serve the public well and to promote greater efficiency in providing financial services. The Board's policies and attitudes are evidenced from its order and statements concerning applications for nonbank expansion.[12]

By 1974, however, regulators became concerned that nonbank expansion could be used by BHCs to avoid regulatory constraints, expropriate the FDIC and thereby impose social costs. Therefore, the Board initiated a "go-slow" policy by denying several applications by major BHCs (including Bank of America, Citcorp, and First Chicago) and requiring BHCs to increase their capital-to-asset ratios. For example, in the denial order of Bank of America Corporation on June 19, 1974 the Board said:

> Such expansions should therefore be permitted on a strong capital base. While the Board recognizes the quality and experience on the applicant's management, the present capital position of the applicant is somewhat lower than what the Board would consider appropriate in light of its recent growth. In such circumstances, the Board would prefer to see funds first used to enlarge the capital position of such organization. (*Federal Reserve Bulletin*, 1974, p. 517)

This denial order by the Board is actually a leverage requirement on the BHC. Although, at the present time, the administration of the BHC Act is a major tool of the Board in enforcing capital adequacy requirements on BHCs, it has not expanded its supervision to the nonbank subsidiaries of BHCs.

The appropriate regulation approach to supervision of BHCs depends on integration within the BHC. There are instances where market value maximization of the holding company is to the detriment of banking subsidiaries. For this reason, several authors such as Orgler and Wolkowitz (1976), Mayne (1978) and Silverberg (1975), emphasize that the BHC should be regarded as a single integrated unit for capital adequacy regulations. Others, such as Black, *et. al.* (1978) suggest that the increased risk of bank failures does not justify regulating BHCs.

Supervising a bank holding company as an integrated unit implies monitoring the activities of nonbank and parent companies that affect the subsidiary bank. Under this regulatory approach the Board's policy toward the nonbank expansion of BHCs depends on any increase in BHC risk resulting from investments in these activities. This is an empirical question, for which a study by Jessee (1976) provides some insights. He applies a cross-sectional comparison of specific types (measures) of risk-taking by affiliated and independent banks. He focuses on four types of risk: capital adequacy, debt leveraging, liquidity risk, and credit risk. For each type of risk (dependent variable), a cross-section equation (model) is estimated. The explanatory variables include: affiliation with a BHC (dummy variable), the level of other types of risk, and other specific variables (e.g., size, net income, growth). His sample includes 171 observations from New York State (121 independent banks and 50 affiliated banks) and 66 observations in New Jersey (46 independent banks and 20 affiliated banks). Jessee applies similar tests to examine the level of risk inherent in consumer finance subsidiaries and independent consumer finance companies. His sample includes 29 firms (of which 14 are affiliated with BHCs). He concludes:

> We have seen empirical proof that banks (and nonbank firms) affiliated with bank holding companies are pursuing riskier operating practices than independently owned institutions. In the areas of capital adequacy, debt leveraging and liquidity, holding company banks have exhibited a desire to assume greater levels of risk. On the other hand, there is some evidence that this group of banks has actually been extending less risky—or, at least, no more risky—loans and employing lesser amounts of long-term debt in their capital structure than independent banks. (P. 251)

Jessee's approach suffers from several methodological deficiencies. (1) The cross-section risk comparison ignores possible adverse effects on the BHC (i.e., double leveraging). (2) The *ad hoc* cross-section models attempt to identify and measure different types of risk, but omit several sources of risk, such as net open position in foreign currencies and the maturity gap between assets and liabilities. (3) The validity of the assumed linear tradeoffs among different types of risk is questionable.[13] (4) The use of accounting numbers in empirical studies poses severe problems in general, and in particuliar in measuring intra-corporate (BHC) transactions. Therefore, his procedure does not seem to be an adequate substitution for measuring the overall risk in firms.

In summary, the nonbank expansion following the 1970 Amendment to the Bank Holding Company Act could be regarded as a part of a more general wave of mergers in the economy. Therefore, the general theories of mergers and acquisitions can be applied to an analysis of BHC expansion into nonbank activities. Accordingly, the expected advantages resulting from forming a BHC are analyzed within the suggested normative model presented in Chapter II. These advantages include, first, the joint production of financial services using the same input, especially information; second, the possible shifting of resources among subsidiaries in accordance with their investment opportunities, at transaction costs lower than those borne when external claims are issued; third, a decrease in expected costs of bankruptcy by permitting greater service and geographical diversification.

It should be recalled, however, that the banking industry is regulated; hence, the expansion into other fields could be motivated by incentives such as avoiding regulatory constraints and expropriating the FDIC (e.g., by double leverage and other practices discussed in this chapter). It might be argued that the foregoing rationales often underlie the behavior of bank regulators and motivate regulatory actions such as the Board's denial orders and a "go-slow" policy.

Chapter V presents an empirical analysis designed to evaluate the consequences of BHCs' acquisition on stockholders' wealth in light of the normative model of the individual bank decision-making process. The implied effects and corresponding motivations of regulatory behavior are also derived from the analysis.

Chapter V

Bank Holding Companies' Acquisition of Nonbank Firms, the Federal Reserve Board's Decision Orders and Stockholder Returns: Empirical Analysis

With the enactment of the 1970 Amendment to the Bank Holding Company Act, each bank holding company which intends to acquire a nonbank firm has to apply to the Federal Reserve Board for approval. This chapter analyzes the effects of these acquisitions on the profitability and riskiness of bank holding company stocks as well as the effects of the Board's decision. Alternative hypotheses and their empirical implications are discussed and then tested using stock market data. Finally, the results are interpreted and operational implications for the regulation of BHCs are derived.

V.1 Alternative Hypotheses of BHCs' Acquisitions of Nonbank Activities

The discussion in Chapter IV suggests alternative rationales for the expansion of BHCs into nonbank activities. The following hypotheses seem most applicable to BHCs' expansion into nonbank activities: production (synergy) efficiency, monopolistic power, investment incentive, and market share expansion. These hypotheses and their empirical implications are discussed next.

A. The Production (Synergy) Hypothesis

This hypothesis states that there are gains from the combined production of banking and closely related (complementary) financial services resulting from the nonbank expansion of BHCs. The implication is that a BHC benefits from such an acquisition, and its announcement releases new positive information about the BHC; thus, it is expected that stock prices of the acquiring BHCs will rise to reflect this new information. The production efficiency hypothesis does not predict the impact of such expansion on the riskiness of the BHCs' shares.[1]

B. The Monopolistic Hypothesis

This hypothesis suggests that nonbank acquisitions result in monopolistic market power and that monopoly rents are generated. The monopolistic hypothesis is discussed by Ellert (1976), and Dodd and Ruback (1977), and applied to bank mergers by Boczar (1976). Because of the BHCs' low market shares in most of their nonbank activities (see Holland, 1975) and because of competition among banks and nonbank firms, it is unlikely that such acquisition will result in monopolistic market power. BHCs and their affiliates supply, however, a major portion (60 percent) of mortgage banking services, as of June 30, 1977 (see Rice, 1978). Therefore, if there is any monopolistic power associated with nonbank acquisitions, it should be in this market. In addition, the potential monopoly power of BHCs in nonbank markets has played an important role in the Board's decisions, particularly with respect to the acquisition of mortgage companies, so this area of nonbank expansion should be examined especially carefully. The monopolistic hypothesis has the same empirical implications for stockholders as the synergy hypothesis; however, the two hypotheses have very different implications for regulators (as discussed in Section V.2).

C. The Investment Incentive Hypothesis

This hypothesis states that nonbank expansion of BHCs increases their riskiness and indirectly increases the risk of bank failure; this comes about because nonbank expansion by BHCs via subsidiaries permits them to avoid the regulators and thereby to increase their riskiness. The increase in risk in the BHCs' shares raises the market value of these shares essentially by expropriating the FDIC. Alternatively, the structure of deposit insurance and the expected regulatory extension of protection to nonbank subsidiaries may lead BHCs to undertake risks in their banks and in nonbank subsidiaries without incurring an appropriate (market-determined) insurance premium.[2] The empirical implications of this hypothesis are that nonbank expansion increases the market value of the BHCs' shares and increases their variance-risk.

D. The Market Share Hypothesis

This hypothesis states that BHCs seek to maintain or increase their nonbank market shares, taking explicitly into consideration the growth activities of other banking organizations in their state (market). In other words, a BHC will react to the nonbank expansion of competing banks by making acquisitions and *de novo* expansions into nonbank activities in order to preserve its relative standing (share) in the market. This hypothesis originally was advanced to explain bank mergers (see Alhadeff and Alhadeff, 1955, and Moyer and Sussana, 1975); however, it might also explain the expansion of BHCs into nonbank activities. It is important to note that the market share hypothesis is not necessarily consistent with maximizing the owners' wealth and hence requires additional considerations of management-owner conflict. The empirical implication of the market share hypothesis is that a BHC stockholder earns less than or equal to normal returns from nonbank expansion. This hypothesis makes no prediction as to how the riskiness of the BHCs' shares is affected by such expansion.

The empirical implications of the effect of the expansion of BHCs into nonbank activities are summarized as follows:

Effect of Nonbank Expansion on BHCs' Stock Prices

Hypothesis	Abnormal Returns	Change in Variance-Risk
Production (synergy) efficiency	positive	undetermined
Monopolistic	positive	undetermined
Investment incentive	positive	increase
Market share	non-positive	undetermined

V.2 Alternative Hypotheses of the Board's Denial Orders of BHC Applications for Expansion into Nonbank Activities

Section 4(c)(8) of the Bank Holding Company Act requires the Board to determine whether a proposed nonbank acquisition serves the public interest before such an acquisition is approved. Therefore, analysis of the Board's decisions ought to be based on the same set of hypotheses discussed in Section V.1. In practice, the Board's implementation of the public benefit test was based mainly on two criteria: (1) increased competition and (2) the effect of a proposed acquisition on the capital adequacy consideration.[3] Accordingly, the Board's denial orders serve two basic purposes for bank regulation: (1) to prevent monopoly power (as perceived by the Board) in "permissible" nonbank markets, and (2) to act as a major tool for capital adequacy regulation. The following discussion is based on the analyses presented in Chapters III and IV of this study.

A. The Capital Adequacy Requirement Hypothesis

The Board's denial orders are frequently stated as a capital adequacy requirement imposed on a BHC (e.g., see the Bank of America case cited in

Chapter IV). Therefore, it is reasonable to assume that the Board's decision (order) is based on an overall evaluation of the BHC's risk, and not just on the specific acquisition in question. This should be true because the acquired firms are very small relative to the size of the BHCs. In fact, in almost all cases, the acquired firm's assets are less than 5 percent of the total assets of the BHC.[4] Thus, the denial orders convey information to the market about regulatory intentions to further constrain the BHCs' decision-making processes. Unanticipated increases in capital adequacy requirements are expected to decrease a BHC's market value, as discussed in Chapter III.[5] Also, any foregone profit opportunity that results from not acquiring the specific nonbank corporation will lead to a reduction in a BHC's market value. The empirical implications of the Board's denial order are, therefore, a reduction in a BHC's market value and a decrease in its variance-risk, i.e., the Board's action had its intended effect, as discussed in Chapter III.

B. The Adverse Effects Hypothesis

Under this hypothesis the Board's denial orders also are aimed at decreasing the banks' risk. The banks reactions, however, foil the Board's attempt and therefore no decrease in the bank variance-risk is expected (as discussed in Chapter III). The expected reduction in a BHC's market value resulting from the Board's denial order is the same as under the previous hypothesis. The empirical implications of this hypothesis, therefore, are that prices of these BHCs' shares will fall (thereby reflecting the new negative information provided by the denial order) but that their overall risk will not decrease.

C. Increased Competition Hypothesis

The increased competition hypothesis states that the denied acquisitions are those that have the potential to result in monopolistic tendencies. In most cases, the Board's orders include an analysis of potential monopolistic power; this is especially true of acquisition of mortgage companies. For example, such analysis uses a concentration ratio in the relevant markets as indicators of monopolistic power. The implication of the increased competition hypothesis is that unanticipated denial orders are expected to decrease a BHCs' market value. The negative returns reflect the foregone expected monopoly rents generated at the time that such an acquisition is announced. The hypothesis implies no significant change in the variance-risk due to denied acquisitions.

D. The Zero Impact Hypothesis

This hypothesis states that the denied acquisition provides no profit opportunity *per se*. It also states that the denial orders do not convey new information to the stock market since they are part of other widely known actions undertaken by regulators. This hypothesis is also consistent with the argument that regulators, in practice, cannot impose any constraint (see Pletzman, 1970). The rationale for the Board's policy under this hypothesis can be explained by the imperfect agent argument advanced in Chapter III. This argument states that regulators seek to maximize their own utility through their decisions. However, the specific measures which serve this objective and their implications need to be identified. Based on the results in this study, this issue is discussed further in Section V.6.

The empirical implications of the effects of the Board's denial orders are summarized as follows:

Hypothesis	Abnormal Returns	Changes in Variance-Risk
Capital adequacy requirement	negative	decrease
Adverse effects	negative	not significant
Increased competition	negative	not significant
Zero impact	not significant	not significant

V.3 Methodology and Estimation Procedures, Data Sources and Sample Selection

Table 5-1 indicates BHCs' expansion in the primary permissible categories of nonbank industries during the period January 1, 1971 to September 10, 1977.

The sample of nonbank firm acquisitions by bank holding companies used in the current study is obtained from the Weekly Federal Reserve Release H.2.: *Applications and Reports Received or Acted on and All Other Actions of the Board,* and from the *Federal Register.* These publications include all applications for acquiring nonbank firms according to section 4(c)(8) of the BHC Act. For those cases where there is a date of announcement that precedes the application date, such information is obtained from the *Wall Street Journal Index*; this date is used to indicate the week of the announcement (AW).[6] Otherwise the announcement week is determined by the application date.

The sample includes the acquisitions for which:

(1) The application was submitted during the period 1971-76.

(2) The total assets of the acquired firm exceeded $5 million. Denied acquisitions are included in this sample regardless of their assets.

Table 5-1

**Proposed Acquisitions of Nonbank Firms by BHCs Processed by the Board
January 1, 1971—September 10, 1977**

Type of Acquisition	Universe			This Study Sample[b]		
	Number approved	Number denied	Total	Number approved	Number denied	Total
Fiduciary & Trust	11	1	12			
Mortgage Banking	80	10	90	18	7	25
Leasing	17	3	20	1	2	3
Financial Advisory Services	20	3	23	0	1	1
Insurance Agencies	129	15	144	2	0	2
Insurance Underwriting	50	—	50			
Finance Company[a]	118	12	130	29	9	38
Data Processing	19	1	20			
Factoring	8	1	9	3	0	3

[a] Includes: general, commercial, consumer, insurance premium, mobile homes and agricultural finance companies. The distinction between the different types is not well defined. Where offices of an acquired finance company are separate corporate entities each is treated by the Board as a separate case. In this table, such a case is considered as one acquisition.

[b] A major part of this sample of applications (62 percent) was announced and the Board's decision was enacted during the period January 1, 1971 through December 31, 1973.

Table 5-1 (Continued)

Proposed Acquisitions of Nonbank Firms by BHCs Processed by the Board
January 1, 1971—September 10, 1977

Type of Acquisition	Universe			This Study Sample[b]		
	Number approved	Number denied	Total	Number approved	Number denied	Total
Community Development	—	2	2			
Industrial Banking	15	3	18	0	1	1
Savings & Loan Association	2	3	5	0	1	1
Others	11	—	11			
Total	480	54	534	53	21	74
DeNovo Entries into All Activities[c]	3,092		3,092			

[c] These figures do not necessarily reflect the initial entry of a holding company into a nonbank activity through formation of a new company. A substantial proportion of these entries simply involves setting up an additional office by an existing company.

Source: "Bank Expansion Quarterly," Vol. XXI, December 1977, Charter Golembe Assoc., Inc., Washington, D.C.

(3) Stock prices of the acquiring BHC were available at least 40 weeks before the application.

This selection procedure yielded a sample of 74 applications (21 of them
denied) by 58 bank holding companies. (This is the largest sample available.)[7]
Table 5-1 provides the breakdown of this sample into different types of
activity. This sample includes 25 applications (7 of them denied) for acquiring
mortgage companies. The average period between the announcement of an
intended acquisition and the Board's decision is 29.4 weeks. The shortest
period is one week and the longest is 106 weeks. The stock prices used in this
study came from two sources: the CRSP (Center for Research in Security
Prices, University of Chicago) file of daily returns, and the Daily Stock Prices
Record Over-The-Counter (Standard and Poor Corporation); for the latter, bid
prices are used.

A. Methodology

The study considers the effects of nonbank acquisition on the profitability of
the acquiring banks and on their risk. The methodologies for measuring these
effects are as follows:

1. Measurement of Abnormal Returns

To measure abnormal returns, some equilibrium model of expected returns on
assets that define "normal" return should   used. The deviation of the weekly
return on a stock from its expected normal return, given the return earned by
the market portfolio (market-wide changes) represents the abnormal return.
The methodology employed presumes that security returns are distributed
multivariate normally, and the following market model is used:

$$(23) \quad \tilde{R}_{jt} = \alpha_j + \beta_j \tilde{R}_{mt} + \tilde{\varepsilon}_{jt},$$

where:

$\tilde{R}_{jt}$ = rate of return of security j over week $t, j = 1, \ldots, N$

$\tilde{R}_{mt}$ = rate of return on the CRSP value weighted index of all New York
Stock Exchange common stock over week t, which is assumed to
reflect the market portfolio of risky assets,

β_j = covariance $(\tilde{R}_{jt}, \tilde{R}_{mt})$/variance $(\tilde{R}_{mt})$,

$\tilde{\varepsilon}_{jt}$ = distu⌐ ⌐ e term of security j at week t, $E(\tilde{\varepsilon}_{jt}) = 0$, and

α_j ≡ $E(\tilde{R}_j) - \beta_j E(\tilde{R}_m)$.

In empirical studies the market model is interpreted as follows[8]: the return on
the market portfolio, $\tilde{R}_{mt}$, is assumed to capture the effects of the

common factor that affects the returns on all securities, whereas the disturbance term, $\tilde{\varepsilon}_{jt}$, captures the firm-specific effects on security j returns. The coefficient, β_j, is the systematic risk of security j; it measures the sensitivity of the returns on security j to market movements. In this view, part of the return on security j, $\beta_j\tilde{R}_{mt}$, is presumed to be caused by market-wide variations in returns.

The market equilibrium model is used to determine whether bank stockholders realized abnormal returns in the weeks surrounding the earliest announcement date of a bank's intended acquisition of a nonbank firm. The "announcement week" is denoted by AW. Week $AW - 1$ is one week before the announcement, and week $AW - 50$ is 50 weeks before the announcement. The "decision week" is defined as the week during which the Board's decision is released and denoted by DW. Week $DW + 1$ is one week after DW and week $DW + 50$ is 50 weeks afer DW.[9] Abnormal returns, $\hat{\varepsilon}_{jw}$, are defined as the difference between realized security returns and the estimated equilibrium returns predicted from the market model. N_w is the number of banks for which an estimate of $\hat{\varepsilon}_{jw}$ can be obtained at week w. Then, in any week w (where for each bank w is measured relative to one of the event weeks, AW or DW), the average weekly residual across sample member (AR_w) is:

$$(24) \qquad AR_w = \frac{1}{N_w} \sum_{j=1}^{N_w} \hat{\varepsilon}_{jw}, \; \hat{\varepsilon}_{jw} = R_{jw} - \hat{\alpha}_j - \hat{\beta}_j R_{mw}.$$

These average residuals are summed over event time to obtain cumulative average residuals (CAR).

$$(25) \qquad CAR_{K,L} = \sum_{w=K}^{L} AR_w,$$

where K and L specify the time period relative to AW or DW. The average weekly residual and cumulative average residuals can be interpreted as the abnormal performance in the returns of sample members during the relevant period.

The analysis refers to seven holding periods surrounding the events, as follows:[10]

(1) "Pre-period (50 weeks); $AW - 55$ through $AW - 6$,

(2) "Pre-announcement" period (6 weeks); $AW - 5$ through AW,

(3) "Post-announcement" period (3 weeks); $AW + 1$ through $AW + 3$,

(4)   "Processing" period (length varies among applications); AW + 1
      through DW,

(5)   "Pre-decision" period (3 weeks); DW − 3 through DW − 1,

(6)   "Post-decision" period (6 weeks); DW through DW + 5,

(7)   "Post" period (50 weeks); DW + 6 through DW + 55.

The above sequence of holding periods can be represented as follows:

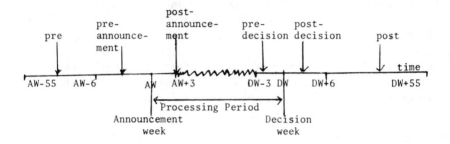

The parameter ($\hat{\alpha}$, $\hat{\beta}$ in Eq. 23) estimation periods are an extended "pre"
period (60 weeks) AW-65 through AW-6 and an extended "post" period (60
weeks), DW + 6 through DW + 65.

The acquisition of a nonbank firm may also induce a shift in the
systematic risk (slope coefficient) of the BHC. As a precaution against nonstationarity in the coefficient parameters, residuals from the market model are
calculated using two sets of coefficients ($\hat{\alpha}_j$ and $\hat{\beta}_j$ in Eq. 23) one estimated
before the announcement of the intended acquisition (extended pre period) and
the second after the Board's decision is announced (extended post period). For
any firm in this sample, two separate market models are estimated. The $\hat{\alpha}_j$ and
$\hat{\beta}_j$ coefficients which are estimated from the data before the announcement
week (AW-65 through AW-6) are used to calculate residuals for the three
periods which precede and surround the announcement week and for the
processing period. The $\hat{\alpha}_j$ and $\hat{\beta}_j$ coefficients estimated from data after the
decision week (DW + 6 through DW + 65) are used to calculate residuals for the
three periods which surround and follow the release of the Board's decision.
For all firms $\hat{\alpha}_j$ and $\hat{\beta}_j$ are estimated using a minimum of 34 weeks and a
maximum of 60 weeks, in all cases data are excluded for the pre-announcement
and the post-decision periods as well as for the processing period. These weeks

are excluded since the dates that the information about intended acquisition and the Board's decision became publicly available are not known precisely.[11] The estimated $\hat{\alpha}_j$ and $\hat{\beta}_j$ are then used to calculate AR and CAR as described. Finally, probability t-tests on the statistical significance of estimated residuals patterns are calculated and reported in the next section.

2. Measurement of Shifts in Risk

The conventional measure of owner risk is the variability of the rate of return to capital. The measure of the variability using accounting data results in systematic biases; therefore, security market prices are used. For the purposes of this study changes in the variance of returns on a BHC's stock serve to measure changes in the risk of bank failure. The *direction* and *significance* of changes in this risk are of interest; however, an estimation of the probability of bank failures is beyond the scope of this study. The estimated variance of returns according to the market model (Eq. 23) is:

$$(26) \qquad \text{Var}(\tilde{R}_j) \; = \; \beta_j^2 \text{Var}(\tilde{R}_m) + \text{Var}(\tilde{\varepsilon}_j) \text{ and } \text{cov}(\tilde{\varepsilon}_j, \tilde{R}_m) \; = \; 0.$$

where:

$\text{Var}(\tilde{R}_j) \; = \;$ variance of returns of security j,

$\text{Var}(\tilde{R}_m) \; = \;$ variance of returns of the market portfolio of risky assets, and

$\text{Var}(\tilde{\varepsilon}_j) \; = \;$ variance of the disturbance term of security j.

The term $\beta_j^2 \text{Var}(\tilde{R}_m)$ in Equation (26), a component of $\text{Var}(\tilde{R}_j)$, is caused by market-wide variables, whereas $\text{Var}(\tilde{\varepsilon}_j)$, a component of the variability of return on security j, is due to variables more specific to the prospects of security j. To test for possible changes in risk, the estimated variance of return of each security for the period before the week of announcement is compared to the variance of returns estimated for the period following the Board's decision. An F test is used to test the significance of these differences. Then, the properties of the distribution of these risk measures across banks in the subsamples of denied and approved applications are compared in the periods before announcement and following the Board's decision. In cases where a change in the variance does occur, it is important to examine whether this change is caused by firm-specific effects or is merely due to a change in the market-wide factors. Therefore the behavior of the components of the variance of returns on security should be analyzed, i.e., $\beta_j^2 \text{Var}(\tilde{R}_m)$ (the systematic market risk) and $\text{Var}(\tilde{\varepsilon}_j)$ (the residual unsystematic risk) are examined. To test for possible changes in the variance of returns of the market portfolio of risky assets and the variance of the disturbance term, an F test similar to the one used before for the returns of securities is employed for the same time periods.

Finally, to test for possible systematic risk shifts, the following regression is run for each security in the sample.[12]

$$(27) \qquad R_{jt} = a_j + a_j'D_t + b_jR_{mt} + b_j'D_tR_{mt} + e_{jt}.$$

These regressions are run using 120 weeks of data, the extended pre period plus the extended post period (60 weeks before the first event and 60 weeks after the second event), excluding the pre-announcement and the post-decision periods as well as the processing period. The dummy variable, D_t, is set equal to zero for the extended pre period and equal to unity for the extended post period. The t-statistic on the coefficient, b', is used to test for risk shifts. A significant negative t-statistic indicates a decrease in β_j and a significant positive t-statistic indicates an increase in β_j after the Board's decision is released.

V.4   Empirical Results

The results of abnormal returns are presented in Section A, and for risk shifts in Section B below.

A. Abnormal Returns

The results of abnormal returns realized by BHC stockholders in the weeks surrounding the announcement of an intended acquisition and the Board's released decision on a BHC's application are summarized in Tables 5-2 through 5-5 and in Figures 5-1 and 5-2. Two summary measures of abnormal returns are obtained, the cumulative average residuals (CAR) and the average weekly portfolio residuals (AR). As explained in Appendix 5A, the portfolio t-statistic used in this study indicates whether the average of the weekly standardized residuals differs statistically from zero. Since 15 out of the 74 securities studied show evidence of significant risk shifts (see Table 5-8), the residuals calculated for the market model use two sets of coefficients, one estimated before the announcement and the second after the Board's decision as discussed in Section V.3.

The data are divided into two subsamples. Mortgage company acquisitions are analyzed as a group because the Board's decision on applications to acquire these companies emphasizes that a proposed acquisition may have implications for potential monopolistic power. Their approach is affected by the large portion of the mortgage banking services supplied by BHCs and their affiliates, and by the fact that the acquired mortgage companies are among the largest in the industry. Finance companies comprise 76 percent of the balance of the sample. Since Rice (1978) found the nonmortgage companies to be fairly homogeneous, they are analyzed together. The results for the non-mortgage sample are presented in Tables 5-2 and 5-3, and for the mortgage sample in Tables 5-4 and 5-5.

Seven separate periods are of special interest for analyzing the effect of an intended acquisition and the Board's decision. These periods correspond to the following time intervals:

(1)   Three periods that precede and surround an announcement: the pre-period (AW − 55 through AW − 6), the pre-announcement period (AW − 5 through AW), and the post-announcement period (AW + 1 through AW + 3).

(2)   The period during which an application is processed: AW + 1 through DW.[13]

(3)   Three periods that surround and follow a decision: the pre-decision period (DW − 3 through DW − 1), the post-decision period (DW through DW + 5), and the post-period (DW + 6 through DW + 55).

The three-week post-announcement period (AW + 1 through AW + 3) is considered separately to test the efficiency with which the market responds to the economic information (if any) conveyed by an intended acquisition. The three-week pre-decision period (DW-3 through DW-1) is considered in order to test whether there was a leakage of information to the market prior to the Board's decision. The event weeks AW and DW are not considered separately since the dates when the information about the intended acquisition and the Board's decision became publicly available are not known precisely. (Also the data do not show abnormal returns in the event weeks that are different from the five-week period which precedes the announcement and the five-week period which follows the decision.)

The cumulative average residuals, the portfolio average residuals, and the t-statistics for these periods are shown in Tables 5-3 (non-mortgage applications) and 5-5 (mortgage applications). The plots of the cumulative average residuals for the non-mortgage applications (Fig. 5-1) and mortgage acquisitions (Fig. 5-2) present an overall view.

1. Findings

a. Periods that Precede and Surround an Announcement

The results show that stockholders of each group of BHCs, classified according to the type of acquisition applications, earned, on average, normal returns (as predicted from the market model) over the three periods that precede and surround an announcement. The cumulative average residuals for these periods are of small magnitudes, and they do not differ significantly from zero. Two

Table 5-2

Nonmortgage Applications:
Percentage Weekly Average Residuals (AR),
Cumulative Average Residuals (CAR), and Sample Size (N_w)
for All (49) Applications and Two Subgroups, Denied (14) and Approved (35)

Week	All Applications			Denied Applications			Approved Applications		
	N_w	AR	CAR	N_w	AR	CAR	N_w	AR	CAR
AW-55	47	0.55	0.55	14	1.23	1.23	33	0.26	0.26
AW-45	48	−0.31	1.83	14	−0.28	7.00	34	−0.32	−0.31
AW-35	49	0.41	0.81	14	1.21	8.00	35	0.09	−2.15
AW-25	49	−0.45	−0.19	14	−0.56	5.43	35	−0.40	−2.52
AW-15	49	0.16	0.38	14	−0.19	2.52	35	0.30	−0.38
AW-6	49	−0.09	−0.31	14	−0.65	−0.08	35	0.13	−0.49
AW-5	49	−0.24	−0.55	14	0.58	0.50	35	−0.57	−1.06
AW-4	49	0.19	−0.36	14	−1.36	−0.86	35	0.82	−0.24
AW-3	49	−0.28	−0.64	14	−0.51	−1.37	35	−0.19	−0.43
AW-2	49	0.40	−0.24	14	−0.27	−1.64	35	0.67	0.24
AW-1	49	0.24	0	14	−0.15	−1.79	35	0.39	0.63
AW[a]	49	−0.59	−0.59	14	−0.49	−2.28	35	−0.63	0
AW+1[b]	48	−0.09	−0.68	14	1.24	−1.04	34[d]	−0.64	−0.64
AW+2	48	0.31	−0.37	14	0.68	−0.36	34	0.16	−0.48
AW+3	48	0.08	−0.29	14	0.88	0.52	34	−0.26	−0.74
AW+4 through DW-4[c]	49		(−5.38)	14		(−13.71)	35		(−2.71)
DW-3[b]	48	−0.63	−6.01	14	−0.83	−14.54	34[d]	−0.55	−3.26
DW-2	48	−0.06	−6.07	14	−0.41	−14.95	34	0.08	−3.18
DW-1	48	0.46	−5.61	14	1.95	−13.00	34	−0.15	−3.33

[a] AW is the week during which an announcement of a BHC's intended acquisition of the nonbank firm is made. DW is the week during which the Board's decision on a BHC's application is announced.

[b] AW+1 is the first week following an announcement of a BHC intended acquisition of a nonbank firm. DW-3 is the third week preceding the release of the Board's decision.

[c] Because the length of the processing period varies among applications, the cumulative average residual approach cannot be used over this time interval. A proxy for the movement of the CAR over the period AD+1 through DW (and AW+4 through DW−4) is computed for a portfolio containing securities of all banks that announced their intended nonbank acquisition AW+1 and

Table 5-2 (Continued)

Nonmortgage Applications:
Percentage Weekly Average Residuals (AR),
Cumulative Average Residuals (CAR), and Sample Size (N_w)
for All (49) Applications and Two Subgroups, Denied (14) and Approved (35)

Week	All Applications			Denied Applications			Approved Applications		
	N_w	AR	CAR	N_w	AR	CAR	N_w	AR	CAR
DW[a]	49	0.34	−5.27	14	−0.06	−13.06	35	0.49	−2.84
DW + 1	49	0.01	−5.26	14	−0.42	−13.48	35	0.19	−2.65
DW + 2	49	−0.12	−5.38	14	−0.76	−14.24	35	0.14	−2.51
DW + 3	49	−0.30	−5.68	14	−1.29	−15.53	35	0.10	−2.41
DW + 4	49	−0.02	−5.70	14	−1.96	−17.49	35	0.76	−1.65
DW + 5	49	0.03	−5.67	14	1.43	−16.06	35	−0.54	−2.19
DW + 6	49	0.70	−4.97	14	0.32	−15.74	35	0.85	−1.34
DW + 15	49	0.25	−3.96	14	1.57	−15.74	35	−0.28	0.07
DW + 25	49	0.47	1.25	14	1.62	−13.19	35	0.01	6.35
DW + 35	49	−0.15	0.92	14	0.44	−13.85	35	−0.38	6.16
DW + 45	49	0.34	−0.65	14	0.26	−14.36	35	0.37	4.15
DW + 55	49	−0.28	−2.27	14	0.56	−16.40	35	−0.62	2.69

holding these securities until the end of DW. The average period between AW + 1 through DW of applications are as follows: all applications 29.3 weeks; denied applications, 40.6 weeks; and approved applications, 24.8 weeks.

[d] This group includes an acquisition having only one week between AW and DW. This acquisition is deleted from this portfolio for the periods AW + 1 through AW + 3 and DW-3 through DW-1. Because the total processing time for seven applications is six weeks, the length of both the post-announcement period and the pre-decision time are determined to be three weeks each.

Table 5-3

Probability Tests on the Residuals of BHCs that Applied to Acquire Non-Mortgage Companies

Portfolio Formation Period	AW − 55[a] through AW − 6	AW − 5 through AW	AW + 1 through AW + 3	AW + 1[b] through DW	DW − 3 through DW − 1	DW through DW + 5	DW + 6 through DW + 55
A. 49 Cases of Non-mortgage Applications							
Cumulative Average Residuals	−0.31	−0.28	0.30	−4.68	−0.23	−0.06	3.40
Average Portfolio Residuals[c]	−0.01	−0.05	0.10	−0.16	−0.08	−0.01	0.07
Portfolio t-statistic[d,e]	−0.58	0.37	0.19	−1.95***	−0.54	−2.51**	−1.18
B. 14 Denied Non-mortgage Applications							
Cumulative Average Residuals	−0.08	−2.20	2.80	−10.78	0.71	−3.06	−0.34
Average Portfolio Residuals	−0.002	−0.37	0.93	−0.27	0.24	−0.51	−0.01
Portfolio t-statistic	−0.83	−0.75	2.08**	−1.14	0.38	−2.79*	−1.51

[a] Notice that not all securities are included in the portfolio during this entire period (i.e., AW-55 to AW-5, see also Table 5-2). Therefore, the CAR for the entire sample is not necessarily the average of the CAR of its subsamples.

[b] The average portfolio residual for this period for all applications is: —4.68/29.3 = —0.159 per week; for the group of denied applications —10.78/40.6 = —0.268, and for the group of approved applications − 2.84/24.8 = − 0.114.

[c] These are the weekly average portfolio residuals during this holding period, i.e., the CAR for this period divided by the number of weeks.

[d] The portfolio t-statistic is from equation 5A-6 in the Appendix.

[e] As noted by Dodd and Ruback (1977), the standardized portfolio average residuals upon which the t-statistics are based are not identical to the average residuals in Table 5-2. It is possible for the

Table 5-3 (Continued)

Probability Tests on the Residuals of BHCs that
Applied to Acquire Non-Mortgage Companies

Portfolio Formation Period	AW − 55[a] through AW − 6	AW − 5 through AW	AW + 1 through AW + 3	AW + 1[b] through DW	DW − 3 through DW − 1	DW through DW + 5	DW + 6 through DW + 55
C. 35 Approved Non-mortgage Applications							
Cumulative Average Residuals	− 0.49	0.49	− 0.74	− 2.84	−0.62	1.14	4.88
Average Portfolio Residuals	− 0.01	0.08	− 0.25	− 0.11	−0.21	0.19	0.10
Portfolio t-statistic	− 0.29	0.88	− 0.83	− 1.84***	−0.97	—1.30	− 1.59

abnormal returns (as measured by the CAR) and the t-statistics to be of opposite sign since the standardizing process results in the assignment of non-uniform weights to the individual residuals (four such reversals occur in Table 5-3).

   * Significant at 1 percent level (two-tailed test)
  ** Significant at 5 percent level (two-tailed test).
*** Significant at 10 percent level (two-tailed test).

Capital Adequacy Requirements

Table 5-4

Mortgage Applications:
Percentage Weekly Average Residuals (AR), Cumulative Average Residuals (CAR), and Sample Size (N_w) for All (25) Applications and Two Subgroups, Denied (7) and Approved (18)[a]

Week	All Applications			Denied Applications			Approved Applications		
	N_w	AR	CAR	N_w	AR	CAR	N_w	AR	CAR
AW-55	24	−0.52	−0.52	7	−0.53	−0.53	17	−0.52	−0.52
AW-45	25	−1.24	−1.51	7	−0.42	3.45	18	−1.55	−3.53
AW-35	25	−0.20	0.81	7	−0.01	4.55	18	−0.27	−0.73
AW-25	25	−1.36	2.28	7	−0.72	1.16	18	−1.61	2.63
AW-15	25	−0.38	2.71	7	−1.50	−0.84	18	0.05	4.00
AW-6	25	0.06	0.28	7	−0.84	−2.21	18	0.41	1.16
AW-5	25	−0.31	−0.03	7	−0.77	−2.98	18	−0.13	1.03
AW-4	25	−0.51	−0.54	7	0.57	−2.41	18	−0.93	0.10
AW-3	25	0.21	−0.33	7	1.02	−1.39	18	−0.10	0
AW-2	25	0.09	−0.24	7	−1.39	−2.78	18	0.66	0.66
AW-1	25	1.02	0.78	7	0.93	−1.85	18	1.06	1.72
AW	25	0.11	0.89	7	1.12	−0.73	18	−0.29	1.43
AW+1	25	−1.22	−0.33	7	−1.26	−1.99	18	−1.20	0.23
AW+2	25	0.68	0.35	7	1.68	−0.21	18	0.30	0.53
AW+3	25	0.78	1.13	7	0.91	0.60	18	0.72	1.25
AW+4 through DW-4	25		(−7.92)	7		(−4.16)	18		(−9.37)
DW-3	25	−1.26	−9.18	7	−2.02	−6.18	18	−0.97	−10.34
DW-2	25	−0.13	−9.31	7	0.80	−5.38	18	−0.48	−10.82
DW-1	25	0.25	−9.06	7	0.76	−4.62	18	0.05	−10.77
DW	25	−0.03	−9.09	7	−1.57	−6.19	18	0.57	−10.20
DW+1	25	−1.68	−10.77	7	−1.75	−7.94	18	−1.65	−11.85
DW+2	25	−0.10	−10.87	7	−0.21	−8.15	18	−0.06	−11.91
DW+3	25	0.38	−10.49	7	−1.40	−9.55	18	1.07	−10.84
DW+4	25	−1.31	−11.80	7	1.18	−8.37	18	−2.27	−13.11
DW+5	25	−0.85	−12.65	7	0.09	−8.28	18	−1.22	−14.33

Table 5-4 (Continued)

**Mortgage Applications: Percentage Weekly Average Residuals (AR),
Cumulative Average Residuals (CAR), and Sample Size (N_w)**

Week	All Applications			Denied Applications			Approved Applications		
	N_w	AR	CAR	N_w	AR	CAR	N_w	AR	CAR
DW + 6	25	− 1.16	− 13.81	7	− 0.01	− 8.29	18	− 1.60	− 15.93
DW + 15	25	1.60	− 9.55	7	3.28	− 1.66	18	0.94	− 12.16
DW + 25	25	− 0.10	− 11.17	7	− 2.01	− 5.80	18	0.64	− 13.24
DW + 35	25	− 0.96	− 11.87	7	− 0.68	− 4.72	18	− 1.07	− 14.63
DW + 45	25	0.18	− 10.73	7	− 3.48	− 5.72	18	1.10	− 12.66
DW + 55	25	2.12	− 10.58	7	1.48	− 3.17	18	2.37	− 13.44

[a] See notes to Table 5.2.

[b] The average periods between AW + 1 through DW are as follows: all applications, 32.6 weeks; denied applications, 33.6 weeks; and approved applications, 32.2 weeks.

Table 5-5

Probability Tests on the Residuals of BHCs that Applied to Acquire Mortgage Companies[a]

Portfolio Formation Period	AW − 55 through AW − 6	AW − 5 through AW	AW + 1 through AW + 3	AW + 1 through DW	DW − 3 through DW − 1	DW through DW + 5	DW + 6 through DW + 55
A. 25 Cases of Mortgage Applications							
Cumulative Average Residuals	0.28	0.61	0.24	− 9.98	− 1.14	− 3.59	2.07
Average Portfolio Residuals	0.01	0.10	0.08	− 0.31	− 0.38	− 0.60	0.04
Portfolio t-statistic	− 0.10	− 0.01	0.14	− 2.31**	− 0.97	− 3.68*	− 0.94
B. 7 Denied Mortgage Applications							
Cumulative Average Residuals	− 2.21	1.48	1.33	− 5.46	− 0.46	− 3.66	5.11
Average Portfolio Residuals	− 0.04	0.25	0.44	− 0.16	− 0.15	− 0.61	0.10
Portfolio t-statistic	− 0.61	0.70	0.52	− 0.77	0.54	− 1.94***	− 0.22
C. 18 Approved Mortgage Applications							
Cumulative Average Residuals	1.16	0.27	− 0.18	− 11.63	− 1.40	− 3.56	0.89
Average Portfolio Residuals	0.02	0.04	− 0.06	− 0.36	− 0.47	− 0.59	0.02
Portfolio t-statistic	0.12	− 0.67	− 0.12	− 2.59**	− 1.45	− 3.03*	− 1.07

[a] See notes to Table 5-3.

[b] The average portfolio residuals for all mortgage applications are: $-9.98/32.6 = 0.306$ percent per week; for the group of denied mortgage applications $-5.46/33.6 = -0.162$; and for the group of approved mortgage applications $-11.63/32.2 = -0.361$.

* Significant at 1 percent level (two-tailed test).
** Significant at 5 percent level (two-tailed test).
*** Significant at 10 percent level (two-tailed test).

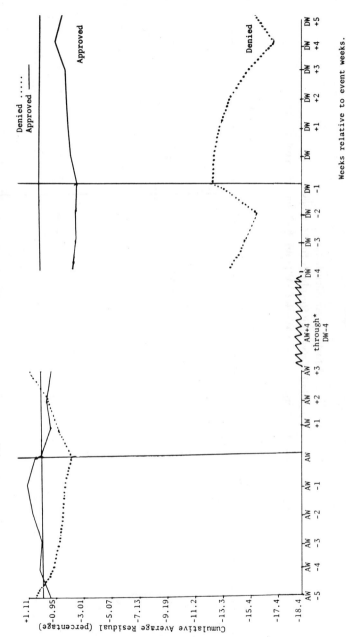

Figure 5-1

Non-Mortgage Applications:
Cumulative Average Residuals for 16 Weeks
Surrounding the Announcement Week (AW) and the Decision Week (DW)

*The length of this period varies among applications.

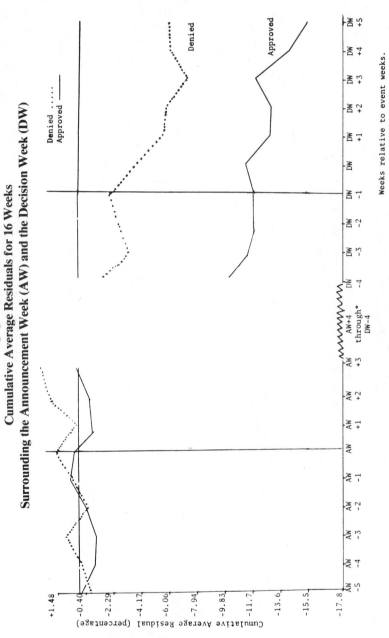

Figure 5-2

Mortgage Applications:
Cumulative Average Residuals for 16 Weeks
Surrounding the Announcement Week (AW) and the Decision Week (DW)

subgroups, however, offer exceptions. First, as shown in Table 5-3, stockholders of the BHCs whose nonmortgage applications were denied earned, on average, significant (probability <0.05) positive abnormal returns (CAR of 2.80 percent) during the post-announcement period (AW + 1 through AW + 3). To test whether these abnormal returns reflect a diffusion of information about an intended acquisition, this period is extended to include the pre-announcement period (AW-5 through AW). The CAR during the extended nine-week period is insignificant and of small magnitude (t-statistic of 0.20, CAR of 0.60). Furthermore, the negative CAR during the pre-announcement periods are inconsistent with the hypothesis that the positive abnormal returns during the post-announcement period reflect diffusion of positive information about the acquisition. Second, as shown in Table 5-5, stockholders of BHCs that were denied mortgage acquisitions earned insignificant ($t<0.70$) abnormal returns (CAR) of 1.48 over the pre-announcement period and 1.33 percent over the post-announcement period. Thus, they indicate a total abnormal return of 2.81 percent during the nine weeks surrounding the week of announcement, the abnormal returns in each subperiod are not significantly different from zero.

b. Period During Which an Application is Processed

The second time interval covers the weeks following the announcement of the application through the week of the Board's decision. Because the length of this period differs among applications, the cumulative average residual approach cannot be used over this time interval. A proxy for the movement of the CAR between these dates can be obtained from the portfolio approach as discussed in note c of Table 5-2. The negative CAR during this period is of relatively large magnitude. As shown in Table 5-3, stockholders of the BHCs with denied non-mortgage applications realized negative returns (CAR of − 10.78), but such returns are not significantly different from zero. Stockholders of the group of approved non-mortgage applications earned significant (probability <0.10) negative abnormal returns (CAR of − 2.84). The returns to stocks of the approved group, though, are of small magnitude compared to the denied group. The results over this period for the group of mortgage applications (see Table 5-5) show that stockholders of the denied application group earned negative returns (CAR of − 5.46), but these returns are not significantly different from "normal" returns. The approved mortgage applications sustained significant (probability <0.05) negative abnormal returns of large magnitude (CAR of − 11.63).

c. Periods that Precede and Surround a Decision by the Board

The third time interval covers the three periods that surround and follow the date the Board's decision rules are enacted. The performance during the pre-decision period shows no obvious or significant pattern that would indicate leakage of information about the Board's decision. During the post-decision period, stockholders of BHCs that were denied non-mortgage acquisition sustained significant (probability <0.01) abnormal losses (CAR of -3.06) (see Table 5-3). Conversely, approved non-mortgage acquisitions realized normal returns during this period. Stockholders of BHCs who were denied mortgage acquisitions realized CAR that average -3.66 percent, significant different from zero at the 10 percent level (see Table 5.5). Where mortgage applications were approved, the abnormal negative returns are similarly negative, -3.56, but even more significantly different from zero (probability <0.01). These returns continue the preceding significant CAR of this group.

Finally, during the period of 50 weeks starting from the sixth week after the Board's decision is announced, stockholders of all classes earned returns that were normal in the sense that they were not significantly different from the average weekly returns that could be earned on a similarly risky portfolio of stocks.

The main findings of the abnormal returns results are summarized below:

(1) Stockholders of a BHC that announced an intended acquisition of a nonbank firm earned normal returns during the three periods that precede and surround the announcement. This indicates that the pre-announcement returns of BHCs that intended to acquire nonbank firms are statistically indistinguishable from those of other companies with similar risk characteristics over an extended period before the week of announcement.

(2) Stockholders of BHCs that were denied acquisitions (mortgage and non-mortgage) sustained significant abnormal losses (about -3.5 percent) during the five weeks following the Board's decision.

(3) During the period when an application is processed, the cumulative average residuals of the stocks of BHCs that applied to acquire mortgage companies show an overall, negative return at significant and large probability (<0.05, CAR of -11.63) which continues during the five weeks following the Board's decision.

(4) During the period in which an application is processed, stockholders of BHCs that were denied non-mortgage applications realized insignificant, negative CAR. Stockholders of the group of approved non-mortgage applications realized significant (probability <0.10) negative abnormal returns of relative small magnitude (CAR of -2.84). Interpretation and implications of these results are discussed further in Sections V.5 and V.6.

B. Shifts in Total Variance-Risk

Recall that the total variance of returns is given by:

$$\text{Var}(\tilde{R}_j) = \beta_j^2 \text{Var}(\tilde{R}_m) + \text{Var}(\tilde{\varepsilon}_j),$$

where:

$\text{Var}(\tilde{R}_j)$ is the estimated total variance-risk,
$\beta_j^2 \text{Var}(\tilde{R}_m)$ is the systematic market risk, and
$\text{Var}(\tilde{\varepsilon}_j)$ is the residual unsystematic risk.

The summary statistics of these risk measures, across BHCs during the pre (announcement) and post (decision) periods are presented in Table 5-6. Since the data show almost no difference in the risk shifts between the two samples, statistics for the mortgage and non-mortgage samples are not presented separately.

The sample average total variance-risk ($\text{Var}\tilde{R}_j$) during the extended pre-period ($AW-65$ through $AW-6$) is insignificantly smaller for the denied applications group than for the approved applications group. On the other hand, the sample average total variance-risk in the extended post period ($DW+6$ through $DW+65$) is significantly larger (at 1 percent level) for the denied applications group than for the approved applications group. Furthermore, results in Table 5-6 show that the increase in the average total variance-risk for the denied group is significant at 1 percent level while the shift in the average total variance for the approved group is not significant, even at 10 percent level. These results indicate that, on average, the sample of denied acquisitions experienced a significantly larger increase in total variance-risk than had the approved applications group. In addition, the evidence suggests that the (insignificant) change in the average total variance-risk in the approved applications group is caused by shifts in the market-wide factors $\beta_j^2 \text{Var}(\tilde{R}_m)$ and not by shifts in the average of the firm-specific component $\text{Var}(\tilde{\varepsilon}_j)$; whereas the change in the average total variance-risk in the denied applications is caused by significant shifts, in both of its components. These implications are analyzed further by testing the shifts in risk of each type of acquisition.

The results of estimated shifts in the total variance-risk of returns on BHCs are summarized in Table 5-7. The comparison of the total variance in the extended post period to the total variance in the extended pre period reveals that substantially more BHCs have experienced statistically significant risk increases (59.5 percent) versus (13.5 percent).

There also appear to be a greater proportion of significant increases in the variance of returns on securities for the denied applications group than for the approved applications group. To test whether there is a difference in distribution between these groups, the following hypotheses are set up:

Table 5-6

Sample Statistics of Risk Measures

Statistics	$Var(\widetilde{R}_j)$ Pre[a]	$Var(\widetilde{R}_j)$ Post[b]	$Var(\widetilde{R}_j)$ t-statistic	β_j Pre	β_j Post	β_j t-statistic	$Var(\widetilde{R}_m)$ Pre	$Var(\widetilde{R}_m)$ Post	$Var(\widetilde{R}_m)$ t-statistic	$Var(\widetilde{\epsilon}_j)$ Pre	$Var(\widetilde{\epsilon}_j)$ Post	$Var(\widetilde{\epsilon}_j)$ t-statistic
Denied Applications (21)												
Mean	0.00099	0.00330	5.26*	0.55	0.89	4.09*	0.00045	0.00118	7.11*	0.00085	0.00236	4.70*
Standard Deviation	0.00045	0.00196		0.23	0.31		0.00021	0.00044		0.00032	0.00144	
Maximum	0.00883	0.00219		1.21	1.39		0.00106	0.00172		0.00148	0.00337	
Minimum	0.00036	0.00040		0.07	0.22		0.00025	0.00025		0.00031	0.00052	
Approved Applications (53)												
Mean	0.00144	0.00205	1.62	0.40	0.64	4.26*	0.00065	0.00086	8.49*	0.00118	0.00163	1.23
Standard Deviation	0.00208	0.00179		0.29	0.29		0.00038	0.00043		0.00197	0.00138	
Maximum	0.01443	0.01105		1.29	1.38		0.00154	0.00153		0.01452	0.00837	
Minimum	0.00028	0.00026		0.13	0.15		0.00023	0.00018		0.00029	0.00026	
t-statistic[d]	0.96	−2.63*										

[a] Pre = extended pre (announcement) period, weeks AW-65 through AW-6.
[b] Post = extended post (decision) period, weeks DW + 6 through DW + 65.
[c] For differences in means; extended post period versus extended pre period.
[d] For differences in means of denied and approved applications (assuming common population variance).
* Significant at 1 percent level (two-tailed test).

Table 5-7

Frequency of Changes in the Variance-Risk Var($\tilde{R}_j$) of Weekly Returns for All BHCs[a]

	Significant increase[b]	No significant change	Significant decrease	Total
Denied applications	18 (85.7%)[c]	2 (9.5%)	1 (4.8%)	21 (100%)
Approved applications	26 (49.1%)	18 (34.0%)	9 (16.9%)	53 (100%)
Total	44 (59.5%)	20 (27.0%)	10 (13.5%)	74 (100%)

[a] Changes in risk are estimated by comparing the variance-risk of weekly returns over the extended pre period and the extended post period.

[b] Significant at 1 percent level.

[c] Percentage of all denied cases.

$H_0:. f_{i1} = f_{i2} \quad i = 1, 2, 3$

H_1: at least one of the equalities in H_0 is not satisfied where i is index of (significant) shifts in risk: $1 = $ increase, $2 = $ no change, $3 = $ decrease; j is index of group: $1 = $ denied applications, $2 = $ approved applications, f_{ij} is the frequency of shifts in risk i in group j.

The appropriate test statistic for the above hypothesis is:

$$\chi^2 = \sum_{i=1}^{3} \sum_{j=1}^{2} \frac{(f_{ij} - F_{ij})^2}{F_{ij}}$$

where:

$$F_{ij} = n_j \sum_{j=1}^{2} \frac{f_{ij}}{n_T}$$

$n_j = $ total cases in group j (21 for group 1, 53 for group 2), and

$n_T = $ total cases in this sample (74).

The sample statistic $\chi^2 = 8.38 > \chi^2_{0.95(2)} = 5.99.$[14] Therefore, it can be concluded that the distribution of risk shifts for denied and approved application groups is different, at the 5 percent significant level.

Finally, Table 5-8 presents the joint frequency of change in variance-risk $Var(\tilde{R}_j)$ and its components; the systematic market component $(\beta_j^2 Var(\tilde{R}_m))$ and the residual unsystematic risk $Var(\tilde{\varepsilon}_j)$. The results in Panel A indicate that, during the period examined, the returns on the market portfolio exhibit risk increase. The BHCs' total variance increase, however, can only partially be explained by these market movements. Rather the BHCs' risk increases reflect changes in the firm-specific risk component. Therefore, this implies changes in the BHCs' production-investment activities and leverage position. As noted earlier, however, the frequency of these risk shifts can not be explained by non-bank expansion.

The main findings of the shifts in risk analyses are summarized below:

(1)   Comparison of risk in the extended post period to the risk in the extended pre period reveals that, on average, this sample of BHC stocks exhibits an increase in the variance-risk. The group of denied applications shows a significantly *larger* frequency of risk increase than does the approved application sample.

(2)   Shares of BHCs whose applications were approved had average variance-risk insignificantly different from the group of denied applica-

Table 5-8

Joint Frequency of Changes in Risk Measures

	Significant Increases in $\mathrm{Var}(\tilde{R}_j)$	No Significant Changes in $\mathrm{Var}(\tilde{R}_j)$	Significant Decreases $\mathrm{Var}(\tilde{R}_j)$	Total
A. Joint Frequency of Significant Changes in $\mathrm{Var}(\tilde{R}_j)$ and $\mathrm{Var}(\tilde{R}_m)$				
Significant increases in $\mathrm{Var}(\tilde{R}_m)$	38	4	0	42
No significant changes in $\mathrm{Var}(\tilde{R}_m)$	5	8	1	14
Significant decreases in $\mathrm{Var}(\tilde{R}_m)$	1	8	9	18
Total	44	20	10	74
B. Joint Frequency of Significant Changes in $\mathrm{Var}(\tilde{R}_j)$ and $\beta_j{}^a$				
Significant increases in $\beta_j{}^a$	13	1	0	14
No significant changes in $\beta_j{}^a$	31	19	9	59
Significant decreases in $\beta_j{}^a$	0	0	1	1
Total	44	20	10	74
C. Joint Frequency of Significant Changes in $\mathrm{Var}(\tilde{R}_j)$ and $\mathrm{Var}(\tilde{\varepsilon}_j)$				
Significant increases in $\mathrm{Var}(\tilde{\varepsilon}_j)$	37	2	0	39
No significant changes in $\mathrm{Var}(\tilde{\varepsilon}_j)$	7	16	3	26
Significant decreases in $\mathrm{Var}(\tilde{\varepsilon}_j)$	0	2	7	9
Total	44	20	10	74

a Significant changes in β_j are obtained from Eq. 27.

tions during the extended pre (announcement) period. In contrast, in the extended post (decision) period the denied group has an average variance-risk that is significantly *larger* than the average of the approved acquisition group.

(3)   The frequency of risk shifts in the sample of mortgage company acquisitions is similar to that of the sample of non-mortgage acquisitions.

(4)   The variance-risk shifts in the sample reflect both shifts in the systematic market risk and in the unsystematic residual risk.

V.5   Interpretation of the Results

The results shown in Section V.4 provide evidence that supports or rejects the alternative hypotheses stated earlier.

A. Rationale for Nonbank Acquisitions

The rationale for nonbank acquisitions is analyzed by examining the market reaction in the three holding periods prior to and surrounding the announcement of an intended acquisition. The synergy, investment incentive, and monopolistic hypotheses imply that there are gains from acquiring nonbank firms. Results in Tables 5-2 and 5-4 suggest that, on average, there are no significant abnormal returns associated with the announcement of acquisitions of nonbank firms in this sample. These results are found for all the subsamples considered.

BHCs that applied to acquire mortgage firms show during the pre- and post-announcement periods $(AW-5$ through $AW+3)$ CAR which are not significantly different from zero. Thus, no evidence was found of significant monopoly rents generated by the acquiring BHCs. A complementary test of monopolistic power is made by examining the returns on a corresponding mortgage-industry portfolio (excluding companies that were subject to an acquisition application), both to an announcement of an intended acquisition and to the release of the Board's decision (see Appendix 5B for such a test). It is argued that monopoly rents generated by the BHCs should simultaneously result in negative returns to existing mortgage companies.[15] The evidence in Tables 5B-1 and 5B-2 (see Appendix 5B) suggests that stockholders of the corresponding mortgage industry portfolios earned, on average, normal returns during the weeks surrounding an announcement of an intended acquisition $(AW-5$ through AW and $AW+1$ through $AW+3)$. The CAR during these periods are of small magnitude and not significantly different from zero. Furthermore, during the post-decision period of denial orders stockholders of mortgage industry portfolios realize significant negative returns (CAR of -2.99 percent with a t-value of -3.17). Thus, the reaction of mortgage banking industry stocks to such announcements provides no support for the monopolistic hypothesis, further substantiating the results obtained in the analysis of BHCs.

The investment incentive is the only hypothesis that explicitly predicts risk changes that results from a BHC's acquiring a nonbank firm. This hypothesis predicts that nonbank expansion permits bank subsidiaries to avoid regulators, to increase the banks' risks and, hence, to expropriate the FDIC. The results presented in Tables 5-6 and 5-7 suggest that, on average, the sample of BHC stocks used in this study exhibit risk increases following the Board's decision as compared to the period before announcement. The group of denied applications, however, shows a greater frequency of significant risk increase than does the sample of approved applications. Furthermore, this risk increase is not preceded by (associated with) positive abnormal returns. Therefore, on the basis of these results, the investment incentive hypothesis is rejected.

The market share hypothesis suggests that BHC expansion into nonbank activities is aimed at preserving their nonbank market share and thus no gain to stockholders is to be expected. The results are consistent with this hypothesis. However, no evidence of significant loss was found in this sample of acquisitions; thus these investments, *per se*, do not necessarily lead to manager-owner conflicts.

B. The Board's Denial Orders

The rationale for the Board's denial orders and their effect are analyzed by examining the evidence on risk shifts and abnormal returns in the three holding periods surrounding and following the release of the Board's decision. The only large and significant market reaction occurs during the post-decision period (DW through DW + 5). The returns on securities of the BHCs involved are, on average, negative, and the cumulative average residuals amount during this period about -3.5 percent and significantly different from zero. This result is common to both mortgage and non-mortgage groups.

The zero impact hypothesis states that any observed loss around a denial order is independent of the order. That is, this hypothesis implies that the market has an accurate perception of the decision rules actually used by the Board, and any observed losses are attributable to the bad performance of these firms prior to the denial orders (which, however, may affect the Board's decision). This hypothesis is rejected for the following reasons. First, there are significant negative abnormal returns following the Board's denial orders for both groups of acquisitions (as well as for the group of approved mortgage company acquisitions). Second, in the pre-decision and the processing periods the CAR are not significantly different from zero for both groups of denied applications; whereas significant negative abnormal returns are realized by stockholders of approved applications.

The negative returns following the Board's denial orders are consistent with each of the increased competition, capital adequacy, and adverse effect hypotheses. A closer look at the evidence enables one to discriminate between these hypotheses.

The increased competition hypothesis states that acquisition of nonbank firms could generate monopolistic power and denial orders could result in negative returns that reflect a foregone monopoly rent. However, the evidence of market reaction to the announcement of an intended acquisition (non-abnormal returns) is inconsistent with this hypothesis. The significant negative returns on the securities of BHCs that were denied acquisitions of non-mortgage firms further support this conclusion since the low market share of BHCs in these markets (Holland, 1975) is unlikely to result in monopolistic power. This conclusion is reinforced by a closer analysis of the mortgage industry reaction to these denial orders. These findings (see Table 5B-1) are inconsistent with the positive returns predicted by the increased competition hypothesis. Thus, on the basis of these results, this hypothesis is rejected.

The evidence of market reaction to the Board's denial orders is consistent with the capital adequacy and the adverse effect hypotheses. Both hypotheses regard the denial orders as a source of information (unanticipated) to the market about regulatory intentions to further constrain the BHCs' decision-making processes. Thus, these hypotheses imply negative returns to the stock-holders of the banks involved. The capital adequacy requirements and the adverse effect hypotheses differ, however, with respect to the predicted effect of such capital adequacy requirements on a bank's variance-risk. The capital adequacy requirement hypothesis implies a decrease in a bank's overall risk; in contrast, the adverse effect hypothesis does not predict this result. The evidence of risk shifts in this sample, shown in Tables 5-6 and 5-7, suggests that, on average, the sample of denied applications shows significantly larger (compared to those of approved applications) frequencies of risk increases following the Board's decision. Thus, to the extent that the denial orders serve as a signal of the expected imposition of additional capital adequacy requirements, the findings of this study support the adverse effect hypothesis, thereby implying that capital adequacy requirements are ineffective. In fact, the increased variance-risk found implies that the Board's negative action indicated greater risk from future adverse regulatory actions. Or, the action may have served as a signal to the market that the BHC was riskier than had previously been estimated.

C. The Impact of Various Nonbank Investments on BHCs

Each intended acquisition affects the BHC's stockholders' wealth at the initial announcement or prior market knowledge of such an investment. This effect reflects the present value of anticipated future economic rents generated by this acquisition. The evidence in this chapter indicates that the effect of the announcement of BHCs' intended acquisitions of nonbank firms, as perceived from stock price behavior, is not significantly different from zero.

The performance of BHCs' stocks during the processing period is not considered separately. It is assumed that this performance is not directly related to the events examined in this study. However, the performance of each investment affects the realized returns on BHCs' securities during the period it is held. The stock market performance of other (not acquired) mortgage banking companies during holding periods considered in this study is estimated as an indicator of the impact of acquired mortgage banking companies on the parent BHC. The returns on an investment in a portfolio of mortgage banking stocks during holding periods that are equivalent to the sample used in this study are estimated for this purpose (see Appendix 5B). The results show that, on average, returns on investments in mortgage companies were negative during these periods, particularly in the processing period. The results in Table 5B-2 show that, during the processing period, the returns on corresponding mortgage industry portfolios show relatively large negative CAR (-16.79 percent for the denied applications group and -8.25 percent for the approved applications group) that are significantly different from zero. The negative returns for the denied applications group are of larger magnitude than those of the approved applications group.[16] These results are supported by Rice (1978), who provides evidence that investment in mortgage banking during the period 1971 to 1976 had much lower returns than did investment in banking and other nonbank activities. The realized negative returns on mortgage banking investments are expected to affect the parent holding companies according to the weight of such investments in a BHC's total assets. Data on such weights are not available; thus the extent to which investments in mortgage banking contribute to the negative abnormal returns in the sample of BHCs' acquiring mortgage companies can not be examined.[17]

Finally, the nonbank investments had considerable consequences for the parent bank holding company during the period 1971 to 1976. In a few well-publicized instances, cited in Chapter IV, mortgage banking subsidiaries actually precipitated failure of banking organizations. In less extreme cases, mortgage (and other nonbank) subsidiaries sustained substantial losses far in excess of their relative size.

V.6   An Evaluation of Current Regulation of BHCs

Currently the regulation of BHCs is carried out mainly through the processing (decision rules) of their applications to engage in nonbank activities and in the determination of the list of permissible nonbank activities. The Board's decision rules on acquisition applications and the "go-slow" policy initiated by the Board in 1974 are evaluated on the basis of evidence provided in the current study.

A. An Evaluation of the Board's Decision Rules on Applications for Acquiring Nonbank Firms

Section 4(c)(8) of the Bank Holding Company Act states that:

> In determining whether a particular activity is a proper incident to banking or managing or controlling banks the Board should consider whether its performance by an affiliate of a holding company can reasonably be expected to produce benefits to the public, such as greater convenience, increased competition, or gains in efficiency, that outweigh possible adverse effects, such as undue concentration of resources, decreased or unfair competition, conflicts of interests, or unsound banking practices.

An analysis of the sample of acquisitions in this study reveals that nonbank acquisitions, *per se*, cannot explain risk shifts in bank holding companies. The sample of denied acquisitions shows, on average, significant and substantial risk increase compared to the sample of approved applications.[18] Therefore, if the Board attempted to control bank risk ("unsound banking practice" in terms of the Act) through its decisions, it was not effective. However, this evidence does not rule out the possibility that denial orders are an indication of the Board's assessment of a bank's inadequate capital position and that other measures will be taken to decrease a bank's risk.

An examination of the released Board's decisions and of the attached analyses shows that the Board's policy emphasized implications for increased competition in a proposed acquisition. The Board's behavior is in accordance with the guidelines provided by Section 3 of the Act to deny a proposed acquisition if its

> effect in any section of the country may be substantially to lessen competition, or to tend to create a monopoly, or which in any other manner would be in restraint of trade, unless [the Board] finds that the anticompetitive effects of the proposed transaction are clearly outweighed in the public interest by the probable effect of the transaction in meeting the convenience and needs of the community to be served.

Further, the fact that the Board approved all applications for *de novo* expansion supports such an assumed policy, since the major difference is that *de novo* expansion has apparently greater potential impact on competition.

The Board's approach, however, cannot be justified on a theoretical basis nor on the basis of empirical evidence. Evidence that there is considerable competition among banks in supplying banking services has been documented (see Benston 1973 and Meltzer 1967 for reviews). Such competition among banks and from nonbank firms clearly would prevent any monopoly rent in nonbank fields. The empirical evidence from the sample of mortgage acquisitions studied and complementary evidence for the mortgage banking industry (see Appendix 5B) do not confirm the existence of monopoly rents associated with the acquisition of mortgage companies.[19] Thus, it seems that the Board put too much effort into unimportant aspects of the 1970 Amendment and failed to serve properly the public's best interests, as defined by the Bank Holding Company Act.

An alternative hypothesis is that regulators maximize their own welfare, (as discussed in Chapter III), rather than the public's best interest. The wording of the Bank Holding Company Act may lead the regulator to believe that he is evaluated by his capability to prevent *any* monopolistic power in the financial services industry. Given this political environment, he would have an incentive to deny an acquisition that give BHCs any apparent potential monopolistic power. The fact that all *de novo* applications were approved by the Board is consistent with this hypothesis.[20]

B. An Evaluation of the Board's "Go-Slow" Policy

The Board considered the overall impact of nonbank expansion on bank risk during the first half of 1974 and instituted a "go-slow" policy toward holding companies' expansion. They stated:

> The Board has previously expressed the view that at this time bank holding companies generally should slow their rate of expansion into new activities and should direct their energies toward strengthening existing operations, particularly where such expansion may be into new activities in which bank holding companies have not previously engaged. That view is especially applicable to bank holding companies applying to acquire companies which are highly leveraged and which would require continuing infusions of capital. (*Federal Reserve Bulletin,* 1974, p. 868).

Evidence from stock price behavior is used to estimate risk shifts in the industry between the periods preceding and following the 1970 Amendment. An equally weighted portfolio of a group of 73 bank securities, for which stock prices are available for relevant periods, is constructed. Then three equally weighted portfolios of subsamples of banks are formed. The effects of the 1970 Amendment on the profitability and risk of these groups of banks would have been expected to differ according to their nonbank activities as follows. The first group consists of 33 one-bank holding companies (in December 1970) that were unregulated before the amendment, as discussed in Chapter IV. The second group consists of 25 multibank holding companies that were subject to the Bank Holding Company Act prior to 1970. The third group consists of 15 independent banks.

Two measures of risk are estimated for each portfolio: total variance risk ($\text{Var}\tilde{R}_p$) and systematic risk ($\hat{\beta}_p$), both by use of the market model (Eq. 23). Three periods of equal length are considered:

Period 1: 60 weeks between 18 November 1968 and 5 January 1970;
Period 2: 60 weeks between 2 August 1971 and 22 September 1972; and
Period 3: 60 weeks between 25 September 1972 and 15 November 1973.

The first period ends about one year (50 weeks) before the Amendment was passed (December 31, 1970) to control for the effect of information leakage or for possible market expectation of the forthcoming amendment. The second and third periods are after enactment of the 1970 Amendment and represent periods of extensive nonbank expansion by BHCs. Therefore, any risk shifts that result from such expansion would have occurred during these periods. The results are presented in Table 5-9.

There is evidence of significant and substantial risk increase in all portfolios during the third period as compared to the second period; in contrast, during the second period significant decrease of risk occurs when compared to the first period. Further statistical comparison of the third and first periods shows no significant risk change.

The findings of both risk measures reinforce the conclusion derived from the analysis of risk shifts of each bank in the sample applying for the Board's approval (Table 5-7). BHC expansion into nonbank activities occurred in general during periods of unstable risk in the banking industry. However, these changes in risk are not found to be related to nonbank expansion; the pattern of risk shifts of the three subsamples portfolios are similar. Furthermore, these risk shifts were found to coincide with shifts in the variance-risk of the market portfolio (economy-wide changes). Thus, to a large extent, the risk shift in the banking industry reflects the nonstationarity of the economy. Therefore, if it is further assumed that economy-wide changes are unanticipated and independently distributed over time, regulatory intervention, such as the "go-slow" policy, is based on *ex post* observation and initiated with a time lag. Finally, it is important to note that, on average, the total variance of bank stocks (at least in this sample) indicates that the industry has a lower risk as compared to the economy as a whole; the total variance-risk of each of these groups is lower than the market portfolio and their β_p's are all less than 1. This evidence is consistent with findings of Santomero and Vinso (1977) that inadequate capital or high probability of bankruptcy is not a common characteristic of the industry as a whole, but rather is specific to a small group of problem banks.

Table 5-9

Estimates of Risk Shifts of Portfolios of Bank Stocks

Holding Period Portfolio	Holding Period 1 11/18/68 through 1/5/70	Holding Period 2 8/2/71 through 9/22/72	Holding Period 3 9/25/72 through 11/15/73
Variance of (percentage) returns on the market portfolio	5.41	3.75***	6.37**
All banks (73)			
Systematic risk (β_p)	0.45 (8.99)a	0.25* (3.99)	0.49* (9.86)
Total variance-risk (Var R_p)	1.90	1.09**	2.47*
One-bank holding companies (33)			
Systematic risk (β_p)	0.49 (8.01)	0.23* (3.31)	0.58* (10.56)
Total variance-risk (Var R_p)	2.48	1.23*	3.23*
Multibank holding companies (25)			
Systematic risk (β_p)	0.44 (9.88)	0.22* (3.55)	0.39** (7.39)
Total variance-risk (Var R_p)	1.69	1.05**	2.00*
Independent banks (15)			
Systematic risk (β_p)	0.38 (6.56)	0.32 (4.54)	0.48** (8.13)
Total variance-risk (Var R_p)	1.88	1.53	2.76**

a Parentheses contain t-statistics

  * Change in risk compared to the previous period significant at 1 percent level.
 ** Change in risk compared to the previous period significant at 5 percent level.
*** Change in risk compared to the previous period significant at 10 percent level.

Chapter VI

Summary and Implications for the Regulation of Bank Holding Companies

The major goals of this study are: first, to analyze the impact of current capital adequacy regulations on the decision-making process of individual banks and, thereby, to provide an evaluation of the efficiency of regulatory intervention; second, to examine and test the effects of recently enacted legislation—the 1970 Amendment to the Bank Holding Company Act—on the profitability and risk of holding companies. This second analysis also provides an opportunity to assess the effects of capital adequacy regulation as well as to explore other goals of regulatory behavior.

A model of the individual bank decision-making process is formulated in Chapter II as a basis for subsequently analyzing (in Chapter III) the banking industry under capital adequacy regulation. It is assumed that a bank's objective is maximizing the market value of its outstanding shares. An important input in this maximization process is the existence of significant bankruptcy costs in the banking industry which affect the valuation of claims on the bank and, hence, affect investment and financing decisions taken by the bank. In the model developed, the expected bankruptcy costs are designed to take the form of a safety-first constraint on the lending and financing decisions.

Uncertainty about borrowers' financial condition makes such information a major factor in the production function of services associated with loans. Banks enjoy a relative advantage (e.g., compared to the bond market) in acquiring and analyzing information that reduces screening costs and costs of ownership conflicts (i.e., writing a loan contract, collecting and analyzing information about the borrower, and enforcing the contract). Thus, the economic role of commercial banks in the loan market becomes the production of financial commodities (loans) at lower costs than by other segments in the economy, *cet. par.*

The essence of a bank's financing management is the decision as to what type and volume of financial claims to issue. Three types of claims are considered: deposits, which are an integral part of the transaction services provided by banks; equity capital, which is relatively costly and infrequently issued in comparison with other sources; and borrowing in the money market, which provides the bank with unlimited short-term borrowing opportunities that can be risky because of liquidity considerations. Emphasis is placed on the cost involved in issuing each type of claim and on the interactions between the bank's financing and the investment (lending) decisions.

Regulators are assumed to serve the public's interest by: (1) using their comparative advantage in monitoring bank risk, on the assumption that it is more efficient for the government than for individual depositors to examine banks; and (2) preventing the external diseconomies generated by a loss of public confidence due to bank failure.

The major means used by bank regulators in different countries to effect the aforementioned goals are portfolio (solvency) contraints, bank examination, and deposit insurance. The suggested framework of the individual bank decision-making processes, as developed in Chapter II, is used in Chapter III to analyze the impact of different regulatory schemes on a bank's market value and the social costs involved in implementing these schemes. The analysis suggests that the effectiveness of capital adequacy regulation in those countries that use portfolio constraints depends on regulators' ability to prevent risk increase in the unconstrained activities. In countries that use deposit insurance and portfolio constraints, the danger of loss for most depositors is eliminated; similarly the probability of bank runs is substantially reduced. However, bank stockholders have incentives to increase risks and expropriate the FDIC. The United States' experience suggests that portfolio constraints are effective in protecting the FDIC's funds. But considerations of efficiency and social costs are also required to evaluate different sets of bank regulations.

Two major types of bank regulation costs are distinguished. One is the costs of foregone opportunities to the public and the banks to the extent that portfolio constraints inhibit the efficient allocation of resources. These costs are analyzed by comparing the decision-making process of regulated versus unregulated banks using the model developed in Chapter II. In particular, regulatory constraints result in the following: they (1) require a bank to issue financial claims in a certain (fixed) composition that is unlikely to coincide with the one determined in the unregulated maximization process, thereby imposing larger transaction costs for issuing claims; and (2) restrict a bank's access to some relevant markets. Under conditions of uncertainty concerning customers' activities and performance, economies of scale can be gained from producing a diversified mix of financial services using given information. Hence, regulatory constraints impose production inefficiency.

The second type of bank regulation costs includes the explicit costs of maintaining the regulatory function and the implicit costs of inefficiencies inherent in this process. Bank regulation inefficiencies result from possible conflicts of interest that arise from administration by imperfect agents who maximize their own welfare rather than serve the public's interests, as well as inefficiencies from portfolio regulations. Portfolio constraints deal separately with each type of risk and do not allow substitutions among different types of risk within the general constraint of the probability of bankruptcy; hence, they impose additional social costs.

Recommendations for improvement in the existing regulatory system derived from this analysis are presented in Chapter III. Essentially such recommendations include the elimination of portfolio constraints, and assessment of banks' riskiness through observation of their stock performance. Accordingly, bank regulators can use capital market data to estimate a bank's overall risk and then impose constraints only on banks that are likely to fail.

The growth of bank holding companies (BHCs) and their expansion into nonbank activites following the 1970 Amendment to the Bank Holding Company Act produced an important structural change in the banking industry and stimulated adjustment in the regulatory process. The expansion of banks into nonbank activities could be regarded as a part of a more general wave of mergers in the economy. Therefore, the general theories of mergers and acquisitions can be applied to an analysis of this expansion by BHCs. Accordingly, in Chapter IV, the expected advantages resulting from forming a BHC are analyzed within the model presented in Chapter II. These advantages include: first, the joint production of financial services using the same input, especially information; second, the possible shifting of resources among subsidiaries, in accordance with investment opportunities, at transaction costs lower than those borne when external claims are issued; and, third, a decrease in the expected costs of bankruptcy by permitting greater product and geographic diversification. Since the banking industry is regulated, expansion into other fields could be motivated by incentives to avoid regulatory constraints and to expropriate the FDIC (e.g., by the double leveraging and other practices discussed in Chapter IV). It might be argued that consideration of the foregoing motivations often induced regulatory actions such as the Board's denial orders and "go-slow" policy.

Chapter V presents an empirical analysis designed to evaluate the consequences of BHCs' acquisitions on stockholders' wealth in light of the individual bank's decision-making process. The implied effects and corresponding motivations of the regulators are also derived from this analysis. Four rationales are delineated; three predict that nonbank acquisitions will have a positive impact on the values of acquiring BHC stocks, and the fourth hypothesis states that nonbank acquisitions have a zero or a negative effect on the wealth of the shareholders of the acquiring firms. The positive impact hypotheses are: production efficiency, monopolistic power, and investment incentive. These hypotheses imply that the stock prices of the acquiring BHCs will rise in response to the announcement of an intended nonbank acquisition. However, they yield different implications for bank regulation.

According to the production efficiency hypothesis the stockholders of the acquiring firms realize abnormal returns as a result of efficiency gained in the production and consumption of financial services. These abnormal returns are not gained at the expense of other groups in the economy, but rather indicate an increase in social welfare (the public's best interest as expressed by the 1970 Amendment). According to the other two positive impact hypotheses, stockholders of the acquiring firms also earn above-normal returns. However, these economic rents are earned at least partially at the expense of other groups in the economy. The monopolistic hypothesis states that nonbank acquisitions by BHCs result in monopolistic market power and that monopoly rent is generated at the expense of consumers and other producers of these financial services. The investment incentive hypothesis posits that nonbank expansion increases shareholders' wealth by expropriating the FDIC. Therefore, a BHC and its subsidiaries do not incur an appropriate (market determined) insurance premium for greater risk. In other words, abnormal returns realized by stockholders of the acquiring BHCs reflect merely a redistribution of wealth in the economy, and hence do not necessarily result in an increase in social welfare. Thus, assuming that regulation intends to serve the public's interest, such acquisitions should attract the regulators' attention.

The fourth hypothesis, the market share hypothesis, asserts that BHCs seek to maintain or increase their nonbank market share. This hypothesis predicts that a BHC stockholder earns, at most, normal returns on nonbank investments. As noted earlier, to the extent that those acquisitions involve negative returns they lead to management-owner conflict; however, this conflict *per se* is not a source of concern to the regulators.

In conclusion, under the assumption that regulators serve the public's interest, the investment incentive and monopolistic power hypotheses are the ones that could justify regulatory intervention in such acquisitions.

The hypotheses were tested by examining the market adjusted stock prices of the shares of BHCs that sought to acquire nonbank companies. The sample was disaggregated into mortgage companies and others (particularly consumer finance companies). The analysis revealed that:

(1) Stockholders of a BHC that announced an intended acquisition of a nonbank firm realized normal returns during the period that surrounds the announcement.

(2) The group of denied applications shows a significantly *larger* frequency of risk increase than does the approved application sample.

(3) Stockholders of BHCs that were denied acquisitions sustained significant abnormal losses during the five weeks following the Board's decision.

(4)   Evidence from the mortgage banking industry confirms that mort-
        gage acquisitions did not generate monopoly rents.

The Board's "go-slow" policy adopted by mid-1974 reduced the number
of approved proposed acquisitions on the grounds that the acquisitions represented unacceptable levels of risk. This policy was evaluated by examining the
riskiness of three portfolios of bank shares: one-bank holding companies (prior
to the 1970 Amendment), multibank holding companies, and independent
banks over three 60-week time periods, one before the 1970 Amendment and
two periods following the 1970 Amendment and preceding the "go-slow"
policy initiation. The data reveal that these changes in risk are not related to
nonbank expansion.

The results of these empirical analyses suggest that BHC expansion into
nonbank activities is aimed at preserving their nonbank market share.
However, the data do not indicate that this action is contrary to the interests of
shareholders. Also, the Board's decision rules were not effective measures for
protecting the public's best interest as defined by the 1970 Amendment. To the
extent that the Board's decision rules were used as measures to impose capital
adequacy requirements or were used as a device to indicate insufficient capital
in a bank, they are found to be both ineffective and inefficient. The sample of
denied acquisitions shows significant and substantial risk increase during the
period following the announcement of the Board's decisions. Furthermore,
because regulatory measures other than the denial orders are required to reduce
bank risk, any foregone profit opportunity caused by the denial orders results
in additional costs and inefficiencies.

The Board's concern about monopolistic power in nonbank markets also
seems to be overstated. There is ample evidence of considerable competition
among banks in supplying banking services (see Benston, 1973, and Meltzer,
1967). Also competition from nonbank firms appears to be sufficient to
prevent any monopoly rents in nonbank activities. The empirical evidence from
the sample of mortgage acquisitions studied, and the complementary evidence
from the mortgage banking industry do not confirm the existence of monopoly
rent associated with the acquisition of mortgage companies.

Since the Board's decision rules are not found to serve the public's best
interest, it can be argued that regulators seek to maximize their own welfare.
The fact that all *de novo* applications were approved by the Board implies that
the Board's policy reflects the agency problem discussed in Chapter III. Let us
assume, for example, that the regulator believes that the public (and hence
politicians) are sensitive to the existence of monopoly power (i.e., they use this
indicator to evaluate regulatory performance). Then, the Board's decision
behavior can be explained as maximizing its own welfare. There is no clear
evidence to confirm or to reject this hypothesis, and it is still unclear how the
processing of applications for acquiring firms serves either the public interest or

maximizes regulators' welfare. In addition, substantial direct regulatory costs are involved in the administration of BHC's applications, e.g., analyzing each application, time required for the decision rules by the Board, and the costs of publishing these decisions. The processing of applications also imposes considerable costs on the banks involved. The administration of these applications, *per se,* does not serve any foreseen regulatory purpose and imposes considerable costs. Therefore, the evidence lends support to the recommendation to remove the Board's administration of applications. Then the efficiency gained and risk involved in each nonbank acquisition would be evaluated by the individual banks and by the market place.

This conclusion does not rule out the importance of examining and supervising BHCs. As long as regulators are concerned with bank risk, whatever the basis of this concern, the Board must consider any significant increase in the risk of bank failures that might arise from holding company affiliation. The evidence cited in both Chapters IV and V suggests that nonbank activities may affect the holding companies' performances far beyond their weight in the total assets of the parent company. The evidence from the few cases where losses in nonbank subsidiaries led (or contributed) to the failure of the parent holding company implies that capital adequacy considerations should be based on the evaluation of the entire organization. In particular, a BHC's leverage position is important because the financial position of the affiliated banks does not necessarily coincide with that of the BHCs, i.e., the double leveraging practice discussed earlier.

Finally, the use of stock prices for assessing banks' overall risk and profitability is recommended in Chapter III, and applied for BHCs in Chapter V. These data are preferable to accounting numbers, since the accounting data have systematic biases relative to the economic concepts that they are trying to measure; hence their viability for measuring economic rents and risks is questionable. This is particularly true for measuring intra-corporate transactions among segments of a BHC. The evidence (see Fama, 1976, for a review) which suggests that the capital market is "efficient," in the sense that asset prices continuously "reflect" all available information, implies that stock prices are a useful alternative source of data that regulators can use for measuring changes in the risk and wealth of the shareholders of holding companies.

Appendix 2A

Exposition of the Credit Portfolio Selection Model

This appendix derives the exposition of $\partial \sigma_{p1}/\partial L_i$ and $\partial \mu_{p1}/\partial L_i$ used in Section II.2.

$$(2A\text{-}1) \quad \partial \sigma_{P1}/\partial L_i = 1/2\sigma_{P1}\{L_i^2 r_i^2 \frac{\partial P_i}{\partial L_i}(1-2P_i)+2L_i^2 r_i \frac{\partial r_i}{\partial L_i}P_i(1-P_i)$$

$$+2L_i r_i^2 P_i(1-P_i)+2\sum_{\substack{i=1 \\ j\neq i}}^{N} L_j r_i r_j \,\mathrm{cov}(\delta_i,\delta_j)$$

$$+2\sum_{\substack{j=1 \\ j\neq i}}^{N} L_i L_j r_j \frac{\partial r_i}{\partial L_i}\mathrm{cov}(\delta_i,\delta_j)$$

$$+2\sum_{\substack{j=1 \\ j\neq i}}^{N} L_j r_i r_j \frac{\partial\,\mathrm{cov}(\delta_i,\delta_j)}{\partial L_i}\}$$

where

$$\mathrm{cov}(\delta_i,\delta_j) = E(\delta_i,\delta_j) - E(\delta_i)E(\delta_j)$$

$$E(\delta_i,\delta_j) = Pr(\delta_i = 1, \delta_j = 1)$$

$$= \int_{-\infty}^{L_i r_i - A_i}\int_{-\infty}^{L_j r_j - A_j} f(R_i, R_j)dR_i dR_j$$

$$\frac{\partial E(\delta_i,\delta_j)}{\partial L_i} = r_i \int_{-\infty}^{L_j r_j - A_j} f(L_i r_i - A_i, R_j)dR_j$$

and

$$\frac{\partial P_i}{\partial L_i} = \frac{\displaystyle\int_{-\infty}^{L_i r_i - A_i} f(R_i)d(R_i)}{\partial L_i} = r_i f_i(L_i r_i - A_i)$$

hence

$$\partial E(\delta_i, \delta_j)/\partial L_i = \partial P_i/\partial L_i \int_{-\infty}^{L_j r_j - A_j} f(L_i r_i - A_i, R_j)/f_i(L_i r_i - A_i)\, dR_j$$

$$= \partial P_i/\partial L_i [Pr(\delta_j = 1 | R_i = L_i r_i - A_i)].$$

Inserting into equation (2A-1) and rearranging we obtain:

$$(2A\text{-}2)\quad \partial \sigma_{P1}/\partial L_i = 1/\sigma_{P1}\{L_i r_i^2 P_i[(1/2 - P_i)(1 + \eta_{r_i} + \eta_{P_i}) + 1/2(1 + \eta_{r_i})]$$

$$+ \sum_{\substack{j=1 \\ j \neq 1}}^{N} L_j r_i r_j[(1 + \eta_{r_i})\,\mathrm{cov}(\delta_i, \delta_j)$$

$$+ P_m P_i[(Pr_{(\delta_j} = 1 | R_i = L_i r_i - A_i) - P_j)]\}$$

where:

$$\eta_{r_i} = \partial r_i/\partial L_i \cdot L_i/r_i$$

is the elasticity of interest rate with respect to the loan size (leverage) determined by the market equilibrium; η_{P_i} is the elasticity of the probability of bankruptcy with respect to the loan size (as determined by the distribution of returns on the underlying project); and

$$(2A\text{-}3)\quad \partial \mu_{p1}/\partial L_i = r_i[(1 + \eta_{r_i})(1 - P_i) - \eta_{P_i}P_i] - 1.$$

Appendix 2B

The Individual Bank's
Decision-Making Process

This appendix provides a formal framework for analyzing the individual bank's decision making process. For expository purposes assume that the returns from information on loans are formulated as discussed in section II.2, and that the transaction costs of issuing claims are as discussed in section II.3. The maximization problem is given by:

$$\text{(2B-1)} \quad \text{maximize } (MV - C) = \sum_{i=1}^{N} L_i V_i(L_i) - T_1(C)$$

$$- T_2(F_0) \int_{-D_0}^{F_0} (F_0 - \tau_1) f(\tau_1) d(\tau_1)$$

S.t.

$$\text{(2B-1-1)} \quad \sum_{i=1}^{N} L_i = F_0 + C + D_0$$

$$\text{(2B-1.2)} \quad \mu_{P3} + Z(\alpha) \sigma_{P3} = -C$$

$$\text{(2B-1.3)} \quad L_i \geqslant 0 \qquad i = 1, \ldots, N,$$

Define $G_3 = G_3(L_i, \lambda_i, C, F_0, \lambda_{31}, \lambda_{32})$

$$\text{(2B-2)} \quad G_3 = \sum_{i=1}^{N} L_i V_i(L_i) - T_1(C) - T_2(F_0) \int_{-D_0}^{F_0} (F_0 - \tau_1) f(\tau_1) d(\tau_1)$$

$$+ \lambda_{31}(F_0 + C + D_0 - \sum_{i=1}^{N} L_i) + \lambda_{32}(\mu_{P3} + Z(\alpha) \sigma_{P3} + C) + \sum_{i=1}^{N} \gamma_i L_i.$$

where:

(2B-3) $\quad \mu_{P3} = \sum\limits_{i=1}^{N} L_i[r_i(1-P_i)-1] - F_0\beta(F_0)E(i_f) + \beta(F_0)E(\tau_1 i_f)$

(2B-4) $\quad \sigma_{P3} = [\sum\limits_{i=1}^{N}\sum\limits_{j=1}^{N} L_i L_j r_i r_j \text{ cov }(\delta_i, \delta_j) + F_0^2\beta(F_0)^2 V(i_f)$

$\qquad\qquad + \beta(F_0)^2 V(\tau_1 i_f) - F_0\beta(F_0)^2 \text{cov}(i_f, \tau_1 i_f)]^{1/2}.$

Differentiating (2B-2) with respect to the endogenous variables, and setting

$$\frac{L_i \partial G_3}{\partial L_i}, \frac{\partial G_3}{\partial \gamma_i}, \frac{\partial G_3}{\partial C}, \frac{\partial G_3}{\partial F_0}, \frac{\partial G_3}{\partial \lambda_{31}}, \frac{\partial G_3}{\partial \lambda_{32}},$$

equal to zero yields the following necessary conditions for optimum.

(2B-5.1) $\quad \dfrac{\partial G_3}{\partial L_i} \leqslant 0.$

(2B-5.2) $\quad L_i \left(\dfrac{\partial G_3}{\partial L_i}\right) = L_i[V_i(1+\eta V_i) - \lambda_{31}$

$\qquad\qquad + \lambda_{32}\left(\dfrac{\partial \mu_{P3}}{\partial L_i} + Z(\alpha)\dfrac{\partial \sigma_{P3}}{\partial L_i}\right) + \gamma_i] = 0$

$\qquad\qquad i = 1, \ldots, N$

(2B-6.1) $\quad \dfrac{\partial G_3}{\partial \gamma_i} \leqslant 0$

(2B-6.2) $\quad \dfrac{\partial G_3}{\partial \gamma_i}\gamma_i = 0 \quad i = 1, \ldots, N$

(2B-7) $\quad \dfrac{\partial G_3}{\partial F_0} = -T_2'(F_0)\int\limits_{-D_0}^{F_0}(F_0-\tau_1)f(\tau_1)d(\tau_1) - T_2(F_0)\int\limits_{-D_0}^{F_0}f(\tau_1)d(\tau_1) +$

$$+ \lambda_{32} \left(\frac{\partial \mu_{P3}}{\partial F_0} + Z(\alpha) \frac{\partial \mu_{P3}}{\partial F_0} \right) + \lambda_{31} = 0$$

(2B-8) $$\frac{\partial G_3}{\partial C} = -T_1{'}(C) + \lambda_{31} + \lambda_{32} = 0$$

(2B-9) $$\frac{\partial G_3}{\partial \lambda_{31}} = F_0 + C + D_0 - \sum_{i=1}^{N} L_i = 0$$

(2B-10) $$\frac{\partial G_3}{\partial \lambda_{32}} = \mu_{P3} + Z(\alpha)\sigma_{P3} + C = 0$$

The solution provides: the credit portfolio $(L_i \ldots L_n)$ such that:

(2B-11) $$\frac{V_i(1 + \eta V_i) - V_j(1 + \eta V_j)}{\left(\dfrac{\partial \mu_{P3}}{\partial L_j} + Z(\alpha) \dfrac{\partial \sigma_{P3}}{\partial L_j} - \dfrac{\partial \mu_{P3}}{\partial L_i} - Z(\alpha) \dfrac{\partial \sigma_{P3}}{\partial L_i} \right)} = \lambda_{32}$$

for all $i, j, i \neq j$

(2B-12)   The optimal composition of liabilities (C, F_0) such that:

$$\frac{T_2{'}(F_0) \displaystyle\int_{-D_0}^{F_0} (F_0 - \tau_1)f(\tau_1)\,d(\tau_1) + T_2(F_0) \displaystyle\int_{-D_0}^{F_0} f(\tau_1)\,d(\tau_1) - T_1{'}(C)}{\left(\dfrac{\partial \mu_{P3}}{\partial F_0} + Z(\alpha) \dfrac{\partial \sigma_{P3}}{\partial F_0} - 1 \right)} = \lambda_{32}$$

and

(2B-13)   The optimal size of the bank

$$\frac{V_i(1 + \eta V_i) - V_j(1 + \eta V_j)}{\left(\dfrac{\partial \mu_{P3}}{\partial L_j} + Z(\alpha) \dfrac{\partial \sigma_{P3}}{\partial L_j} - \dfrac{\partial \mu_{P3}}{\partial L_i} - Z(\alpha) \dfrac{\partial \sigma_{P3}}{\partial L_i} \right)} =$$

$$\dfrac{T_2{}'(F_0)\displaystyle\int_{-D_0}^{F_0}(F_0-\tau_1)f(\tau_1)d(\tau_1)+T_2(F_0)\displaystyle\int_{-D_0}^{F_0}f(\tau_1)d(\tau_1)-T_1{}'(C)}{\left(\dfrac{\partial\mu_{P3}}{\partial F_0}+Z(\alpha)\dfrac{\partial\sigma_{P3}}{\partial F_0}-1\right)},\quad V_{i,j}.$$

This solution is further discussed in Section II.4.

Appendix 3A

The Comparative Statics Analysis
of the Direct Chance Constraint

This appendix illustrates the effects of changes in the direct chance constraint on the portfolio of assets and liabilities a bank holds. The model used is the one developed in section II.3. The first-order partial derivations with respect to each of the endogenous variables $(L, C, F, \lambda_{21}, \lambda_{22})$ are:

$$(3A-1) \quad \bar{V} - \lambda_{21} + \lambda_{22}\left(\frac{\partial \mu_{P2}}{\partial L} + Z(\alpha)\frac{\partial \sigma_{P2}}{\partial L}\right) = 0$$

$$(3A-2) \quad -T_2'(F_0)\int_{-D_0}^{F_0}(F_0 - \tau_1)f(\tau_1)d(\tau_1) - T_2(F_0)\int_{-D_0}^{F_0}f(\tau_1)d(\tau_1)$$

$$+ \lambda_{21} + \lambda_{22}\left(\frac{\partial \mu_{P2}}{\partial F_0} + Z(\alpha)\frac{\partial \sigma_{P2}}{\partial F_0}\right) = 0$$

$$(3A-3) \quad -T_1'(C) + \lambda_{21} + \lambda_{22} = 0$$

$$(3A-4) \quad C + D_0 + F_0 - L = 0$$

$$(3A-5) \quad \mu_{P2} + Z(\alpha)\sigma_{P2} + C = 0.$$

Insert the solution of the Lagrangian multiplier λ_{21} from equation (3A-3) and C (equation 3A-4) into the other three equations and assume for simplicity $T_1''(C) = 0$. We are left with three equations in three unknowns (L, F, λ_{22}). To solve for changes in the endogenous variables with respect to change in the direct chance constraint, $Z(\alpha)$, the total derivatives of equations (3A-1), (3A-2), and (3A-3) are taken, yielding:

$$(3A-6) \quad \left(\frac{\partial \mu_{P2}}{\partial L} + Z(\alpha)\frac{\partial \sigma_{P2}}{\partial L} + 1\right)\frac{d\lambda_{22}}{dZ(\alpha)} = -\lambda_{22}\frac{\partial \sigma_{P2}}{\partial L}$$

$$(3A\text{-}7) \quad [-T_2''(F_0)\int_{-D_0}^{F_0}(F_0-\tau_1)f(\tau_1)\,d(\tau_1) - 2T_2'(F_0)\int_{-D_0}^{F_0}f(\tau_1)d(\tau_1)]$$

$$\times \frac{dF_0}{dZ(\alpha)} + \left(\frac{\partial \mu_{P2}}{\partial F_0} + Z(\alpha)\frac{\partial \sigma_{P2}}{\partial F_0} - 1\right)\frac{d\lambda_{22}}{dZ(\alpha)} = -\lambda_{22}\frac{\partial \sigma_{P2}}{\partial F_0}.$$

$$(3A\text{-}8) \quad \left(\frac{\partial \mu_{P2}}{\partial L} + Z(\alpha)\frac{\partial \sigma_{P2}}{\partial L} + 1\right)\frac{dL}{dZ(\alpha)} + \left(\frac{\partial \mu_{P2}}{\partial F_0} + Z(\alpha)\frac{\partial \sigma_{P2}}{\partial F_0} - 1\right)\frac{dF_0}{dZ(\alpha)}$$

$$= -\left(\frac{\partial \sigma_{P2}}{\partial L} + \frac{\partial \sigma_{P2}}{\partial F_0}\right).$$

These simultaneous equations are then solved and yielding:

$$\frac{dF_0}{d|Z(\alpha)|} < 0 \qquad \frac{d\lambda_{21}}{d|Z(\alpha)|} < 0 \qquad \frac{d\lambda_{22}}{d|Z(\alpha)|} > 0.$$

The sign of $\dfrac{dC}{d|Z(\alpha)|}$ and $\dfrac{dL}{d|Z(\alpha)|}$ are not determined *a priori*.

The condition for decreasing loan is:

$$(3A\text{-}9) \quad -\lambda_{22}\frac{\partial \sigma_{P2}}{\partial L}\left(a_{23}{}^2 + \frac{a_{22}}{\lambda_{22}}a_{13}\right) + \lambda_{22}\frac{\partial \sigma_{P2}}{\partial F_0}\cdot a_{13}\left(a_{23} - \frac{a_{22}}{\lambda_{22}}\right) > 0$$

where:

$$a_{13} = \left(\frac{\partial \mu_{P2}}{\partial L} + Z(\alpha)\frac{\partial \sigma_{P2}}{\partial L} - 1\right) > 0.[1]$$

The effect on the probability of bank failure of a dollar increment in equity capital and granting it as a loan is a_{13}.

$$a_{23} = \left(\frac{\partial \sigma_{P2}}{\partial F_0} + Z(\alpha)\frac{\partial \sigma_{P2}}{\partial F_0} - 1\right) < 0.$$

The effect on the probability of bank failure of borrowing an additional dollar from the money market and using the proceeds to decrease a bank's equity capital (e.g., through dividend policy) is a_{23}.

$$a_{22} = -T_2''(F_0)\int_{-D_0}^{F_0}(F_0-\tau_1)f(\tau_1)d(\tau_1) -$$

$$2T_2'(F_0)\int_{-D_0}^{F_0}f(\tau_1)d(\tau_1)<0.$$

The change in marginal transaction costs of borrowing from the money market and the necessary condition for increasing equity capital is a_{22}.

$dC/d|Z(\alpha)| = dL/d|Z(\alpha)| - dF_0/d|Z(\alpha)|>0$, i.e., the substitution between equity capital and borrowed funds outweighs any possible decrease in the size of the loan portfolio.

(3A-10)
$$-\lambda_{22}\frac{\partial\sigma_{P2}}{\partial L}[a_{23}^2 + a_{13}(\frac{a_{22}}{\lambda_{22}}-a_{23})] +$$

$$\lambda_{22}\frac{\partial\sigma_{P2}}{\partial F_0}a_{13}[a_{23}+a_{13}-\frac{a_{22}}{\lambda_{22}}]<0.$$

The meanings of these conditions are further discussed in section III.1.

Appendix 5A

Probability Tests of CAR

The statistical test used in this study is similar to that used by Jaffe (1974), Mandelker (1974), Ellert (1976), and Dodd and Ruback (1977). The test seeks to determine whether estimated residuals are statistically different from zero in a specific period. Since industry and other factors can cause residuals to be correlated across securities in a given period of time, a portfolio of securities is constructed for each *calendar* time.

The portfolio at calendar week T is formed by the following rule. Define EW_j as the event week; for example, the calendar week when the Board's decision on a BHC application is released (DW_j). The BHC is included in the portfolio at T if

(5A-1) $EW_j + L < T < EW_j + U$, $EW_j \equiv$ either AW_j or DW_j,

where L and U are weeks dated relative to the event week. As an example, consider the particular case where $L = AW - 6$, $U = AW - 1$ and $AW_j = 200$. Firm j will be included in the portfolio for calendar weeks 194 through 199. Similarly, the portfolio of week 200 will include all firms that have event AW_j in weeks 201 through 206.

For each firm j in the portfolio at T, the market model is estimated using the previous 60 weeks of data (excluding T); the estimated coefficients $\hat{\alpha}_j$ and $\hat{\beta}_j$ are then used to calculate the residual $\hat{\varepsilon}_j$ for all firms in the portfolio.

The average portfolio residual in that week is given by

(5A-2) $\hat{e}_{pT} = \dfrac{1}{NF_T} \displaystyle\sum_{j=1}^{NF_T} \hat{\varepsilon}_{jT}$,

where NF_T is the number of firms whose residuals qualify for inclusion in portfolio T. The portfolio variability is estimated using the previous 60 weeks of data (excluding T).[1] Average portfolio residuals for each of the 60 weeks before T are calculated as follows:

$$(5A\text{-}3) \quad \hat{e}_{PT,\tau} = \frac{1}{NF_T} \sum_{j=1}^{NF_T} \hat{\varepsilon}_{j,\tau} \text{ for } \tau = T-60, \ldots, T-1.$$

The average portfolio residuals are then used to calculate the standard deviation of the portfolio residuals e_{PT}.

$$(5A\text{-}4) \quad SD_T = \sqrt{\frac{1}{59} \sum_{w=1}^{60} (\hat{e}_{PT,T-w} - \frac{1}{60} \sum_{w=1}^{60} \hat{e}_{PT,T-w})^2}$$

The standardized residual for the portfolio formed at week T is

$$(5A\text{-}5) \quad SP_T = \frac{\hat{e}_{PT}}{SD_T}$$

There will be one standardized portfolio residual for each calendar week. A weighted average of the weekly standardized average portfolio residuals is given by the following t-statistic.

$$(5A\text{-}6) \quad PTS = \frac{\sum_{T=X}^{y} \frac{\hat{e}_{PT}}{SD_T} \cdot W_T}{\sqrt{\sum_{T=X}^{y} W_T^2}} \quad \text{and } W_T = \frac{NF_T}{\sum_{T=X}^{y} NF_T},$$

where x and y are the first and last calendar weeks in which portfolios are formed. The weighting scheme is used by Ellert (1976). It gives more weight to calendar weeks in which there are more firms in the portfolio.

Appendix 5B

The Performance of the Mortgage Banking Industry

The returns on portfolios of mortgage securities are used to examine the following:

(1) The mortgage banking industry reaction to BHCs' announcements of intended acquisitions of mortgage companies;

(2) The performance of mortgage banking companies during the periods considered in this study.

The hypothesis of the mortgage banking industry reaction to an intended acquisition of a mortgage company by a BHC is derived from the monopolistic hypothesis. To the extent that monopoly rents are generated by an acquisition, negative returns to the industry are expected from such an announcement, and positive returns are expected at the time this application is denied (if it is) by the Board (assuming that the Board's decision is not anticipated by the market). The performance of mortgage banking industry portfolios during holding periods identical to the sample used in this study is estimated in order to examine the returns on the investments in mortgage banking that are specific to the acquiring BHCs.

VB.1 Data and Methodology

For each of 25 intended acquisitions of mortgage companies by BHCs in this sample, a corresponding mortgage industry portfolio is formed. The industry portfolio for each intended acquisition consists of all mortgage companies on the CRSP file (excluding companies that were subject to an acquisition application) on which there are sufficient data during the calendar periods surrounding the announcement and the Board's decision (65 weeks before the announcement and 65 weeks following the Board's decision). Consequently, the composition of securities in the mortgage industry portfolio differs among events (calendar time) because of availability of mortgage company stock prices. The largest industry portfolio contains 57 mortgage observations and the smallest portfolio contains 10 securities.

For each event and corresponding industry portfolio in this sample, two separate market models are estimated using the extended pre-period (AW − 65 through AW − 6) and the extended post-period (DW + 6 through DW + 65). AR and CAR across this sample of corresponding industry portfolios are calculated as described in Section V.3, and probability t-statistics are computed for the same holding periods as the sample of acquisitions, as discussed in Section V.4.

VB.2 Results and Analysis

The results of AR and CAR are presented in Tables 5B-1 and 5B-2 and plotted in Figure 5B-1. The evidence suggests that stockholders of the corresponding mortgage industry portfolios earn, on average, normal returns during the weeks surrounding an announcement of an intended acquisition (AW-5 through AW and AW + 1 through AW + 3). The CAR during these periods are of small magnitude and not significantly different from zero. Furthermore, during the six weeks following the release of the Board's denial orders stockholders of industry portfolios realize significant negative returns (CAR of − 2.99 percent with a t-value of − 3.17). On the basis of these results the monopolistic hypothesis can be rejected.

The results show that, during the processing period the returns on corresponding mortgage industry portfolios are negative CAR (− 16.79 percent for the denied applications group and − 8.25 percent for the approved applications group) that are significantly different from zero. Finally, the negative returns on the mortgage industry portfolios during these periods imply negative returns on BHCs' investments in such activities, thereby explaining, to some extent, the negative returns on the sample of applications to acquire mortgage companies.

Figure 5B-1

**Mortgage Industry Portfolio Corresponding to Mortgage Applications:
Cumulative Average Residuals for 16 Weeks Surrounding
the Announcement Week (AW) and the Decision Week (DW)**

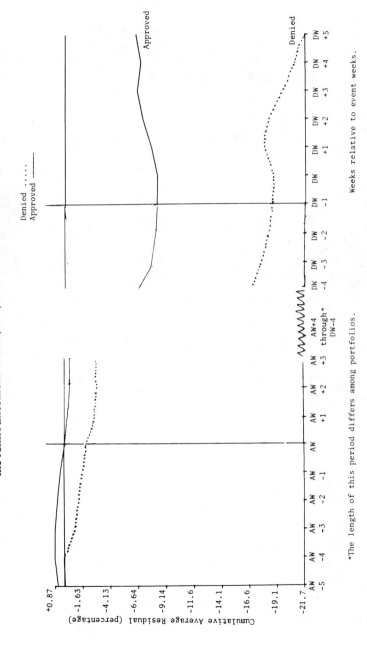

*The length of this period differs among portfolios.

Table 5B-1

Mortgage Industry
Percentage Weekly Average Residual (AR) and Cumulative Average Residuals (CAR) for Portfolios Corresponding to All (25) Mortgage Applications and Two Subgroups, Denied (7) and Approved (18)

Week	All Applications		Denied Applications		Approved Applications	
	AR	CAR	AR	CAR	AR	CAR
AW − 55	−0.11	−0.11	−0.35	−0.35	−0.02	−0.02
AW − 45	0.27	−0.09	0	−1.03	0.38	0.28
AW − 35	0.18	0.34	0.33	0.33	0.12	0.35
AW − 25	−0.33	0.34	−0.30	0.01	−0.34	0.47
AW − 15	0.17	−0.66	−0.17	−1.33	0.30	−0.39
AW − 6	−0.32	−1.60	−0.32	−1.33	−0.32	−1.70
AW − 5	0.41	−1.19	−0.05	−1.38	0.59	−1.11
AW − 4	0.23	−0.96	0.10	−1.28	0.28	−0.83
AW − 3	−0.31	−1.27	−1.04	−2.32	−0.03	−0.86
AW − 2	−0.26	−1.53	−0.33	−2.65	−0.23	−1.09
AW − 1	−0.26	−1.79	−0.29	−2.94	−0.25	−1.34
AW	−0.41	−2.20	−0.39	−3.33	−0.41	−1.75
AW + 1	−0.48	−2.68	−0.67	−4.00	−0.40	−2.15
AW + 2	−0.23	−2.91	−0.15	−4.15	−0.26	−2.41
AW + 3	−0.12	−3.03	−0.10	−4.25	−0.12	−2.53
AW + 4 through DW − 4	(−10.75)		(−16.37)		(−8.65)	
DW − 3	−0.19	−10.94	−1.49	−17.86	0.31	−8.34
DW − 2	−0.90	−11.84	−0.88	−18.74	−0.90	−9.24
DW − 1	−0.88	−12.72	−1.27	−20.01	−0.73	−9.97
DW	−0.05	−12.77	−0.11	−20.12	−0.03	−10.00
DW + 1	0.64	−12.13	0.90	−19.22	0.53	−9.47
DW + 2	0.43	−11.70	−0.41	−19.63	0.76	−8.71
DW + 3	−0.02	−11.72	−1.36	−20.99	0.51	−8.20
DW + 4	−0.52	−12.24	−1.03	−22.02	−0.32	−8.52
DW + 5	0.05	−12.19	−0.96	−22.98	0.43	−8.09

Table 5B-1 (Continued)

Mortgage Industry
Percentage Weekly Average Residual (AR) and Cumulative Average Residuals (CAR) for Portfolios Corresponding to All (25) Mortgage Applications and Two Subgroups, Denied (7) and Approved (18)

Week	All Applications		Denied Applications		Approved Applications	
	AR	CAR	AR	CAR	AR	CAR
DW + 6	1.60	−10.59	2.34	−20.64	−1.31	−6.78
DW + 15	0.29	−7.83	−0.75	−21.41	0.69	−2.63
DW + 25	0.30	−4.55	−0.42	−11.14	0.58	−2.08
DW + 35	0.35	−4.07	1.67	−12.95	−0.16	−0.71
DW + 45	−1.11	−4.89	−1.43	−15.78	−0.98	−1.60
DW + 55	−0.92	−7.85	−2.07	−17.18	−0.47	−4.31

Table 5B-2

Probability Tests on the Residuals of Mortgage Industry Portfolios[a]

Portfolio Formation Period	AW − 5 through AW	AW + 1 through AW + 3	AW + 1 through DW	DW − 3 through DW − 1	DW through DW + 5
A. 25 Mortgage Applications					
Cumulative Average Residuals	−0.60	−0.83	−10.57	−1.97	0.53
Average Portfolio Residuals	−0.10	−0.28	−0.32	−0.66	0.09
Portfolio t-statistic	−1.29	−1.50	−3.49*	−2.74*	−1.81**
B. 7 Denied Mortgage Applications					
Cumulative Average Residuals	−2.00	−0.92	−16.79	−3.64	−2.97
Average Portfolio Residuals	−0.33	−0.31	−0.50	−1.21	−0.49
Portfolio t-statistic	−1.82	−0.50	−3.50*	−2.90*	−3.17*
C. 18 Approved Mortgage Applications					
Cumulative Average Residuals	−0.05	−0.78	−8.25	−1.32	1.88
Average Portfolio Residuals	−0.01	−0.26	−0.27	−0.44	0.31
Portfolio t-statistic	−0.73	−1.67**	−3.33*	−1.60	−0.56

[a] See notes to Tables 5-3 and 5-5.

  * Significant at 1 percent level (two-tailed test).

** Signifcant at 10 percent level (two-tailed test).

Notes

Chapter I

1. Capital is defined as net worth or owner's equity, but in some cases subordinated long-term debt is also included by regulators in capital adequacy considerations. Capital adequacy is a term signifying the amount of equity capital deemed socially optimal by regulators.

2. See Posner (1974) or Peltzman (1976) for a review of economic theories of regulation.

3. An asset is classified as a loss if its expected (by the authorities) realized value is zero. A doubtful asset is defined to be an asset whose expected realized value is less than its book value.

4. It is important to emphasize that regulators attempt to accomplish their goal of maintaining a sound system of banking by broader (than merely leverage constraints) requirements, such as portfolio regulation and deposit insurance. (See discussion in Chapter III.)

5. See Orgler and Wolkowitz (1976) and Pringle (1971) for extensive reviews of the literature on bank capital.

6. Benston (1973) examined the effectiveness of bank examiners in classifying problem banks and found that ". . . the examiners' ability in spotting banks that are likely to fail is far from perfect. . . . Of the 56 banks that failed from January 1950 through April 1971 only 41 percent were classified as problems at the time of the examination approximately one year before failure. Of these, a little more than half were rated serious problem banks. And of the 59 percent not rated as problems, a little more than half were given the highest rating." (p. 43).

Chapter II

1. Most studies in this area treat the individual bank as an investor maximizing expected utility. See for example, Porter (1961), Klein (1971), Michaelsen and Goshy (1967), Fried (1970), Pyle (1972), Blair and Heggestad (1978), Kahane (1977), Kane and Malkiel (1965), Luckett (1970).

2. The assumption of an unregulated industry in this chapter does not rule out the existence of regulations, but rather implies no *direct* intervention in a bank's decision-making process.

3. Akerlof (1970) considers uncertainty and information as major factors determining credit market equilibrium in underdeveloped countries (India is the example he chooses) where differential rates are charged customers according to their quality: ". . . credit is granted

only where the granter has (1) easy means of enforcing his contract or (2) personal knowledge of the character of the borrower." (P. 499)

4. Notice that in a competitive credit market the lender is indifferent to the quality of the loan
   since it is compensated for within the loan agreement. For example, the tighter the loan
   agreement, the lower the interest rate charged on the loan. (See Jensen and Meckling, 1976,
   for a discussion.)

5. The concept of information cost used throughout this study is a static one, where information is purchased or produced at one point in time. Grossman, Kihlstrom, and Mirman
   (1977) introduce a similar concept in an inter-temporal optimization process where information is endogenously generated by a "learning-by-doing" process.

6. In fact most customers have several banking connections (see Benston, 1972, for evidence).
   The advantages of banking with a number of banks are competition among banks and risk
   reduction for banks. On the other hand, this behavior affects economies of scale of information and results in additional transaction costs to customers. Such considerations, however, do not change the nature of the qualitative conclusion derived from the discussion.
   Therefore, for the current discussion it is simply assumed that each customer prefers banking with one bank.

7. It is interesting to note that although other writers such as Luckett (1970), Klein (1971),
   Pringle (1974), and Taggart and Greenbaum (1978), assume that banks possess some comparative advantage in the loan market, they do not justify or identify its nature, its sources,
   or its magnitude.

8. The term project is used throughout this section in a broader sense, i.e., the entire enter-
   prise.

9. By introducing this assumption, the possible existence of investment incentives (see Myers,
   1977) is ignored, i.e., the bank can effectively monitor the investment decision undertaken
   by the borrower.

10. This might occur if the costs of realizing the salvage value of the project are high enough to
    cause the bank to abandon it. This assumption is made for the sake of simplicity of exposi-
    tion.

11. It is important to note that the comparative advantage is bounded by the lower of the two
    following costs: (1) competing banks' costs of acquiring and analyzing information about
    the borrower; and (2) costs associated with transferring the corporation's banking services
    to a competitive bank which allows that bank access to information about the borrower.
    It is reasonable to assume that information costs and, in particular, transaction (trans-
    ferring) costs lead to economies of scale with respect to the size of the loan.

12. The increase in the market value of the bank as a result of the increased risk on the
    credit portfolio should be compared to the increase in expected costs of bankruptcy. It is im-
    plicitly assumed that α and the safety-first constraint are determined in a way that reflects
    these considerations.

13. The endogenously determined benefit from increasing capital should be equal to any costs
    associated with raising new equity capital. However, such considerations require more de-
    tailed analysis of the available financing sources. This is discussed in the next section.

14. Where the collateral is part of the corporation's assets, it merely determines the loss distribution among groups of creditors if the firm goes bankrupt.

15. See Rothschild and Stiglitz (1976) and Jaffee and Russell (1976) for further discussion.

16. Deposit accounts also provide the bank security (collateral). Demanded loans can be called and the deposits "frozen" in quite rapid succession.

17. The discussion is based on Akerlof's (1970) study of the automobile market and Rothschild and Stiglitz's (1976) study of the insurance market. A characteristic peculiar to the deposit market is the fact that depositors have alternative financial markets (assets).

18. Other writers (e.g., Klein, 1971 ; Taggart and Greenbaum, 1978) point out the convenience (lower transaction costs) of having depositors located close to the bank, which limits nonlocal competition and provides the bank with some monopoly power. However, potential and existing competition limits such monopoly power. Hence, a bank's location is assumed to serve as a market-sharing factor rather than a factor creating opportunities to make above-normal returns.

19. This is a rather strong assumption, by which the real output (deposits) is solely determined by demand forces rather than simultaneously through the interaction between demand and supply.

20. Loans can be sold or discounted at the central bank for the market price, but this practice is equivalent to borrowing through the money markets.

21. For a review of the historical development of these methods, see Knight (1969, 1970) and Woodworth (1967). The following discussion is based on their data.

22. The prevalence of this practice is reflected in the literature. In models developed by Porter (1961), Kane and Malkiel (1965), Orr and Mellon (1961), and Baltenspreger and Milde (1976), the stochastic deposit drain was first met by cash balances (primary reserves) and then by selling securities (secondary reserves). In the extreme event of reserve deficiency (i.e., where both primary and secondary reserves prove to be insufficient), adjustment costs are incurred, since the bank is then forced to acquire funds at a high price.

23. It should be noted that the money market instrument is a source of financing or *investment*.

24. The covariability of money market rates and deposits flows is a function of the composition of the deposit portfolio, as discussed later.

25. Monetary policy also affects the behavior of depositors (the deposit flows) and money market rates. However, a detailed discussion of the different approaches to monetary policy and its predicted impact on the banking system's liquidity is beyond the scope of this work. See Lindbeck (1959) and Spencer (1974) for a detailed discussion of the several different channels through which monetary policy affects the economy. The portfolio adjustment process in commercial banks is discussed in Brunner and Meltzer (1972).

26. Loans differ with respect to repayment (installment) schedules (e.g., mortgages, consumer loans, business loans, and lines of credit) and consequently in their effect on the bank's cash flow and liquidity risk. For simplicity, these differences are not considered in the model.

27. The fact that tax subsidy results because interest payments are tax deductible (see Miller, 1977) is ignored in this model.

28. The question of optimal financial structure for a *given* credit portfolio is a trivial one since there is a single composition of equity capital and borrowed funds which complies with the safety-first constraint.

29. The marginal cost of equity capital is assumed to increase, although the marginal direct transaction costs per dollar are decreasing. This is possible since the marginal profit from re-laxing the safety-first constraint decreases as capital increases and the assumed net effect is an increasing schedule of marginal costs.

Chapter III

1.   It is important to note that one way to achieve these purposes is by controlling banks' over-all variance-risk. However, protecting depositors does not necessarily require a low prob-ability of bank failures; alternatively, depositors can be compensated according to the risk they bear.

2.   Risky assets are those so defined by the regulatory authorities. The definitions differ among countries.

3.   Lack of diversification was found (e.g. Benston, 1973) to be a principal cause of bank failures.

4.   The record of past U.S. bank failures (see Benston, 1973) shows the primary causes to have been irregularities, frauds, and self-dealing by officers or employees.

5.   The amount of required reserves represents a realizable (liquid) asset, according to Pierce's (1966) definition, only when bank failure occurs, i.e., their book values can be realized with-in very short time periods.

6.   The reserve requirements are, perhaps, even more associated with the needs of monetary policy than with bank solvency.

7.   In Ireland no more than 10 percent of deposits may be attributed to one customer, and the deposits of the 10 largest depositors must not exceed 40 percent of all the bank's deposits.

8.   One of the requirements for being licensed or registered as a bank is the initial capital re-quirement. In most countries, the requirement that a minimum amount of equity capital be invested by founders of a bank clearly is neither relevant to established banks nor binding to new banks because the requirement is set in nominal (historical) terms.

9.   These differences appear to be caused by different economic conditions among countries, e.g., the degree of development of the stock and money markets. A rigorous analysis of the reasons for such differences is beyond the scope of this study.

10. Included are England, Ireland, Canada, Cyprus, India, Australia, South Africa (until the law was amended in 1963), and Israel.

11. Included are Peru, Argentina, Guatemala, Mexico, Korea, the Philippines, and Thailand.

12. Included are Switzerland, the Netherlands, West Germany, Denmark, Norway, Spain, Belgium, Luxemburg, and Sweden.

13. The United States, Japan, and Greece, which are also included in the sample, do not fit into any of these three categories.

14. Deposit insurance arrangements exist in a few countries (United States, Lebanon, India, and Canada). Other countries (England, Israel) intend to introduce such arrangements in the future. The analysis in this section is based upon the deposit insurance law of the U.S.

15. A monetary rationale for deposit insurance is provided by Mayer (1965), Kreps and Wacht (1971), and Gibson (1972). The deposit insurance cuts the link between bank failures and a reduction in the nation's money supply. The present study concentrates on the micro consequences of bank regulation, and thus does not elaborate this rationale.

16. Merton (1978) shows that the surveillance cost component of deposit insurance premium is, in effect, paid for by depositors.

17. Thus, Kaufman (1975) and Horvitz (1975) argue that the failure of the Franklin National Bank was accelerated by the withdrawals of large (uninsured) deposits.

18. See Barnett, Horvitz, and Silverberg (1977) for policy considerations and statistics concerning the FDIC behavior during the period 1935-1975.

19. Actually, changes in the shadow prices of the safety-first constraint $(d\lambda_{22})$ and of a dollar increment in loans $(d\lambda_{21})$ reflect the interaction among returns to information in asset markets, transaction costs of issuing claims, and the variance-risk of assets and claims.

20. The restriction on the amount of a bank's net open position in foreign currencies is ignored in this analysis. It is assumed that banks prefer to hedge against a net open position through forward exchange contracts, and that the transaction costs involved in these contracts are negligible.

21. It is assumed for simplicity that at time 0 the bank is borrowing at the money market.

22. Other changes include the induced changes in W_i (the size constraint), V_i^*, and the marginal transaction costs of issuing claims (see equations 2B-13 and 22 that state the optimality conditions of unregulated and regulated banks respectively). The effect of these changes on the amount of a single loan and on the credit portfolio is not determined *a priori* and is not considered further here.

23. Note that under current regulatory schemes, banks have incentives to increase the variance-risk of their loan portfolios, as is discussed earlier. However, a bank's behavior only partially offsets the intended effect of regulation, since the bank's overall variance-risk is bounded by its pre-regulation level.

24. This issue is a major source of controversy regarding regulation of bank holding companies and will be discussed further in Chapter IV.

25. In effect, the FDIC provides a put option on a bank's portfolio (see Merton, 1977).

26. Several authors, e.g., Mayer (1965), Meltzer (1967), Peltzman (1970), Merton (1977), and Kareken and Wallace (1978) discuss the investment incentive in detail.

27. For example, the deposit insurance fund amounted to nearly $1.5 billion at the end of 1952, and to nearly $8.0 billion at the end of 1977 (see various issues of the Annual Report of the Federal Deposit Insurance Corporation).

28. This observation, however, does not rule out the existence of adverse effects which increase the probability of bank failure, as a consequence of regulatory intervention.

29. Foreign exchange operations by commercial banks (prior to 1974) may be considered as examples of unconstrained activity. Exchange risk which is associated with foreign exchange operation *per se* does not add any dimension to the issue of capital adequacy, since it can be hedged against by forward exchange contracts without altering the bank's investment and financing decisions. Note, however, that no current commitment of resources is necessary to undertake a forward position. Thus, speculation in forward exchange serves, for some banks, as leverage that permits risk taking (see Rose, 1974, for a description of the Franklin National case). This aspect makes forward exchange speculation attractive for banks that seek a high risk position in order to expropriate the depositors' and FDIC's claims (i.e., investment incentives).

30. As Scott and Mayer (1971) point out, the FDIC currently has a monopoly power that allows it to set the deposit insurance premiums at whatever rate it decides. Scott and Mayer propose instead to allow competition among different federal insurance companies, state-sponsored funds or private insurance companies.

31. The term bank market value as used in this section represents the value of bank shares.

32. For personal and corporate tax considerations and the tax advantage of corporate leverage, see Miller (1977). For a discussion of the costs of conflict of interest, see Jensen and Meckling (1976). For an analysis of flotation costs, see Smith (1977).

33. Notice that such practice could be optimal in unregulated decision-making processes where the amount demanded by a borrower exceeds the optimal amount resulting from the optimization in Section II.2.

34. It is important to note that the bank holding company form of organization and in particular the 1970 Amendment to the Bank Holding Company Act substantially affects the social costs of the regulatory process. This subject is discussed in the following chapter.

35. The tradeoff between regulatory costs and bankruptcy costs of failure is recognized.

36. The public has limited access to information about regulators' (agencies') day-to-day activities. Therefore, the number and magnitude of bank failures is instrumental as an indicator in evaluating regulators' performances.

37. In practice, similar agency problems (and inefficiencies) exist between different levels of the examination process.

38. Regulators can and often do intervene now, despite specified rules.

39. As noted by Benston (1973), in practice charges made by the supervisory agencies are based primarily on a bank's total assets or deposits.

40. Notice that the market prices of bank liabilities (e.g., commercial papers) cannot serve as a proxy for a bank's risk since the expected value of the liabilities is determined also by expectations about the behavior of the FDIC (liquidation vs. merger). For example, it is widely believed that the probability that the FDIC would not let a large bank failure result in liquidation is much lower than for a small bank (i.e., the FDIC also provides some degree of protection to noninsured bank liabilities).

41. For example, see Mayer (1965), Meltzer (1967), and Gibson (1972). Barnett, *et. al.* (1977) review and discuss this and other proposed changes in the deposit insurance system.

42. Notice that under the regulatory process proposed in this section the investment incentive is controlled within the bank's overall variance-risk.

43. In fact, several recently failed banks had stocks traded in the capital market (e.g., Franklin National Bank, Beverly Hills Bancorporation, and National Bank of San Diego).

Chapter IV

1. This is documented in Jessee and Seelig (1977), Chapter 2.

2. See Jessee and Seelig (1977), Table 4-5.

3. For example, on December 12, 1974, Governor Holland testified before the House Committee on Banking and Currency that the Federal Reserve system formally adopted a "slow down" policy for all BHCs (see *Federal Reserve Bulletin,* 1974, p. 838).

4. The hypothesis that nonbank expansion results in monopolistic market power is unlikely and is ignored in the current chapter because of the BHCs' low market share in their nonbank activities, as presented by Holland (1975). BHCs and their affiliates supply, however, a major portion of the mortgage banking services (see Rice, 1978). The potential monopolistic power in this market is examined and tested in Chapter V.

5. The market share hypothesis states that BHCs seek to maintain or increase their nonbank market share. This hypothesis is not necessarily consistent with maximizing the owners' wealth and hence requires additional considerations of management-owner conflict. Such an analysis is beyond the scope of this study. The empirical implications of this hypothesis will be discussed and tested in Chapter V.

6. The so called "double leveraging" practice, where the parent BHC borrows to finance equity investment in banks, raises the important difference between the capital position of the parent BHC and its subsidiaries. To the extent that double leveraging motivates the holding company to issue excessive amounts of debt to meet bank regulators' demands for greater capital in subsidiary banks, the variance-risk of the entity necessarily rises (assuming dependency).

7. See, for example, Black *et. al.,* (1978), Jessee and Seelig (1977), Heggestad (1975), Chase and Mingo (1975), and Silverberg (1975).

8. This is an investment decision for the BHC, where the possible run on banks is an input in this decision.

9. Note that loss to the holding company may not be confined only to the invested equity of the parent in the subsidiary. The contingent liabilities resulting from the intersubsidiaries' dependencies may increase the loss far beyond the BHC investment.

10. Holland (1975) provides evidence for such practice. The 25 largest bank holding companies combined invested $417 million in new equity of their subsidiary banks in 1972 and $371 million in 1973. To support these investments the BHCs issued new equity totalled $140 million and $116 million in 1972 and 1973, respectively, with the resultant difference being an increase in leverage (borrowing).

11. See Jessee and Seelig (1977) for a list of other possible policies.

12. See Jessee and Seelig (1977, Chapter 6) for a detailed analysis of the Board's implementation of the public benefit requirement based on the Board's orders published in the *Federal Reserve Bulletin* between January 1971 and June 1976.

13. These are the tradeoffs among different types of risk determined by the variance-covariance matrix of *each bank* as discussed in Chapter II. These tradeoffs are not likely to be the same cross-sectionally.

Chapter V

1. The diversification hypothesis discussed earlier (in Chapter IV) is a specific form of the synergy hypothesis that also implies a decrease in the variance-risk.

2. Some assumptions about regulatory responses or the dynamics of regulatory behavior need to be made. See the discussion in Chapter III on the extent which such actions by BHCs are limited by regulators.

3. The Board made no rigorous attempt to measure or even to define the efficiency gained ("convenience and needs," in terms of the Act) of a proposed acquisition.

4. Nevertheless, the evidence cited in Chapter IV suggests that nonbank activities may affect holding companies performance far beyond their weight in the total assets of the parent company. Furthermore, the Board might be interested in the cumulative effect of a series of smaller acquisitions.

5. It is more likely to assume that the Board's behavior is expected by the market; however, the precise time and the specific action undertaken by the Board is uncertain, and could vary considerably.

6. Forty-five announcements were obtained from the *Wall Street Journal Index*. These cases are not considered separately. On average, the announcement in the *Wall Street Journal* precedes the week of application by 14 weeks.

7. The use of stock prices is the major constraint on the size of the sample. However, the weight of this sample in total assets of acquired nonbank firms, and hence its importance, goes far beyond its proportionate numbers shown in Table 5-1.

8. See Fama (1976, pp. 63-132) for a discussion of this model.

9. The measurement of abnormal returns surrounding two events was originally presented by Ellert (1976) and closely followed in this study.

10. For reasons discussed later, the events are not considered separately.

11. The five-week periods are considered for possible leakage of information. The length of these periods is decided somewhat arbitrarily.

12. See Dodd and Ruback (1977), p. 358, who used this test.

13. The decision week, DW, is included in this holding period so that the formed portfolio is feasible.

14. Since in the table two entries display very low frequency the χ^2 approximation may be poor. These entries contribute about 40 percent (3.57) to the χ^2 statistic.

15. This is a crude measure of industry reaction since a local market area was not considered for each acquisition. However, most of the mortgage companies involved in this study operate in multistate and even nationwide markets.

16. It could be hypothesized that the negative returns in this industry prior to the enactment of the Board's decisions affected the Board's decision; i.e., the Board tends to deny mortgage (nonbank) acquisition during periods of poor performance in this industry. If this were the case, however, the Board's decisions are based on *ex post* performance, and the positive abnormal returns in the period following the release of the Board's decision (i.e., DW + 5 through DW + 55) provide evidence that indicates the inappropriateness of such an approach, i.e., positive abnormal returns were experienced on industry portfolios corresponding to denied acquisitions (see Table 5B-1).

17. Twenty-one of the intended mortgage company acquisitions in this sample are among the largest 300 mortgage companies, based on volume of permanent mortgages serviced on June 30, 1977 (*American Bankers,* October, 1977).

18. Furthermore, the approved applications group had greater (though not significant) variance-risk than did the denied applications group during the 60-week period before an announcement.

19. As noted earlier BHCs and their affiliates service about 60 percent of all mortgage loans serviced as of 30 June 1977 (Rice 1978). This BHCs' market share is much greater than that of other nonbank markets.

20. *De novo* expansion is subject to the same regulatory procedure as acquisitions. There were no denial orders, however, to *de novo* applications during the reviewed period; i.e., 1971-1977. Thus, such expansion is practically unregulated.

Appendix 3A

1. A sufficient (though not necessary) condition for these results is $a_{13}>0$ which implies the following constraint on α: $|Z(\alpha)|<\sigma_{p2}(1 + \bar{r})/L\bar{r}^2\bar{P}$.

Appendix 5A

1. For each firm j in the portfolio at T, the market model is estimated over weeks $\bar{T} = -120$ through $T-61$ (when data are available). The estimated parameters $\hat{\alpha}_j$, $\hat{\beta}_j$ are then used to calculate residuals for each of the NT_T firms during $T-60$ through $T-1$.

Bibliography

Akerlof, George A., 1970, "The Market for 'Lemons' Qualitative Uncertainty and the Market Mechanism," *Quarterly Journal of Economics,* 84 (August), 488-500.

Alhadeff, David A., and Charlotte P. Alhadeff, 1955, "Recent Bank Mergers," *Quarterly Journal of Economics,* 69 (November), 503-32.

Altman, Edward I., 1968, "Financial Ratios, Discriminant Analysis and the Prediction of Corporate Bankruptcy," *Journal of Finance,* 23 (September), 589-609.

American Bankers Association, 1954, *The Adequacy of a Bank's Funds: A Statement of Principles,* New York, American Bankers Association.

Baltensperger, Ernst., and Hellmuth Milde, 1976, "Predictability of Reserve Demand, Information Costs and Portfolio Behavior of Commercial Banks," *Journal of Finance,* 31 (June), 835-43.

Barnett, Robert E., Paul M. Horvitz, and Stanley C. Silverberg, 1977, "Deposit Insurance: The Present System and Some Alternatives," *Journal of Banking Law,* 94 (April), 304-32.

Baxter, Nevins D., 1967, "Leverage, Risk of Ruin and the Cost of Capital," *Journal of Finance,* 22 (September), 395-404.

Beaver, William H., 1968, "Market Prices Financial Ratios and the Prediction of Failure," *Journal of Accounting Research,* 6 (Autumn), 179-92.

Beighley, Prescott H., John H. Boyd, and Donald P. Jacobs, 1975, "Bank Equities and Investor Risk Perceptions: Some Entailments for Capital Adequacy Regulation," *Journal of Bank Research,* 6 (Autumn), 190-201.

Benston, George J., 1972, "The Optimal Banking Structure: Theory and Evidence from the United States," *Kredit Und Kapital,* 5, 438-76.

_____, 1973, "Bank Examination," *The Bulletin* of the Institute of Finance, Graduate School of Business Administration, New York University, Nos. 89-90 (May).

_____, 1976, "Comments on 'An Analysis of the Capital Required of S&L Associations',"
Change in the Savings and Loan Industry, Proceedings of the Second Annual Conference, Federal Home Loan Bank of San Francisco (December 9-10), 1976, 158-68.

_____, and Clifford W. Smith, Jr., 1976, "A Transaction Cost Approach to the Theory of Financial Intermediation," *Journal of Finance,* 31 (May), 215-23.

Black, Fischer, 1975, "Bank Funds Management in An Efficient Market," *Journal of Financial Economics,* 2 (December), 323-39.

_____, Merton H. Miller, and Richard A. Posner, 1978, "An Approach to the Regulation of Bank Holding Companies," *Journal of Business,* 51 (July), 379-412.

Blair, Roger D., and Arnold A. Heggestad, 1978, "Bank Portfolio Regulation and the Probability of Bank Failure," *Journal of Money, Credit and Banking,* 10 (February), 88-93.

Boczar, Gregory E., 1976, *The Growth of Multibank Holding Companies: 1956-1973,* (Washington, D.C.: Board of Governors of the Federal Reserve System).

Brunner, Karl, and Allan H. Meltzer, 1972, "Money Debt and Economic Activity," *Journal of Political Economy,* 80 (September/October), 951-77.

Buchanan, James M., and Mcolaus T. Tideman, 1974, "Gasoline Rationing and Market Pricing: Public Choice in Political Democracy," Research Paper No. 808231-1-12, Center for Study of Public Choice, Virginia Polytechnic Institute, (January).

Burns, Arthur F., 1974, "Maintaining the Soundness of Our Banking System," Addressed at the 1974 American Bankers Association Convention, Honolulu, Hawaii, October 21.

Chase, Samuel B., and John J. Mingo, 1975, "The Regulation of Bank Holding Companies," *Journal of Finance,* 30 (May), 281-92.

Cohen, Kalman J., 1970, "Improving the Capital Adequacy Formula," *Journal of Bank Research,* 1 (Spring), 13-16.

Cotter, Richard V., 1966, "Capital Ratios and Capital Adequacy," *National Banking Review,* 3 (March), 333-46.

Dodd, Peter, and Richard Ruback, 1977, "Tender Offers and Stockholder Returns: An Empirical Analysis," *Journal of Financial Economics,* 5 (December), 351-73.

Ellert, James C., 1976, "Mergers, Antitrust Law Enforcement, and Stockholder Returns," *Journal of Finance,* 31 (May), 715-32.

Fama, Eugene F., 1976, *Foundations of Finance,* (Basic Books, New York).

Federal Reserve Bulletins, Board of Governors of the Federal Reserve System, Washington, D.C.

Fried, Joel, 1970, "Bank Portfolio Selection," *Journal of Financial and Quantitative Analysis,* 5 (June), 203-27.

Gibson, William E., 1972, "Deposit Insurance in the United States: Evaluation and Reform," *Journal of Financial and Quantitative Analysis,* 7 (March), 1575-94.

Grossman, Sandford J., Richard E. Kihlstrom and Leonard J. Mirman, 1977, "A Bayesian Approach to the Production of Information and Learning by Doing," *Review of Economic Studies,* 44 (October), 533-47.

Heggestad, Arnold A., 1975, "Riskiness of Investments in Nonbank Activities by Bank Holding Companies," *Journal of Economics and Business,* 27 (Spring), 219-23.

_____, and John J. Mingo, 1975, "Capital Management by Holding Company Banks," *Journal of Business,* 48 (October), 500-505.

Hodgman, Donald R., 1963, *Commercial Bank Loan and Investment Policy,* Champaign, Illinois: Bureau of Economic and Business Research, University of Illinois.

Holland, Robert C., 1975, "Bank Holding Companies and Economic Stability," *Journal of Financial and Quantitative Analysis,* 10 (November), 577-87.

Horvitz, Paul M., 1975, "Failures of Large Banks: Implications for Banking Supervision and Deposit Insurance," *Journal of Financial and Quantitative Analysis,* 10 (November), 589-601.

Jaffee, Dwight M., and Thomas Russell, 1976, "Imperfect Information, Uncertainty, and Credit Rationing," *Quarterly Journal of Economics,* 90 (November), 651-66.

Jaffe, Jeffrey F., 1974, "Special Information and Insider Trading," *Journal of Business,* 47 (July), 410-28.

Jensen, Michael C., and William H. Meckling, 1976, "Theory of the Firm: Managerial Behavior, Agency Costs and Ownership Structure," *Journal of Financial Economics,* 3 (October), 305-60.

Jessee, Michael A., 1976, "An Analysis of Risk-Taking Behavior in Bank Holding Companies," Ph.D. dissertation, University of Pennsylvania.

_____, and Steven A. Seeling, 1977, *Bank Holding Companies and the Public Interest,* (Lexington Books, Lexington, Massachusetts).

Kahane, Yehuda, 1977, "Capital Adequacy and the Regulation of Financial Intermediaries," *Journal of Banking and Finance,* 1 (October), 207-18.

Kane, Edward J., and Burton G. Malkiel, 1965, "Bank Portfolio Allocation, Deposit Variability and the Availability Doctrine," *Quarterly Journal of Economics,* 79 (February), 113-34.

Kareken, John H., and Neil Wallace, 1978, "Deposit Insurance and Bank Regulation: A Partial-Equilibrium Exposition," *Journal of Business,* 51 (July), 413-38.

Kaufman, George G., 1975, "Preventing Bank Failures," Center for Capital Market Research, University of Oregon, Eugene, (January).

Klein, Michael A., 1971, "A Theory of the Banking Firm," *Journal of Money, Credit and Banking,* 3 (May), 205-18.

Knight, Robert E., 1969-1970, "An Alternative Approach to Liquidity," *Monthly Review Federal Reserve Bank of Kansas City,* Part I, December 1969, 11-21; Part II, February 1970, 11-22; Part III, April 1970, 3-12; Part IV, May 1970, 10-18.

Kraus, Alan, and Robert H. Litzenberger, 1973, "A State-Preference Model of Optimal Financial Leverage," *Journal of Finance,* 28 (September), 911-22.

Kreps, Clifton H., and Richard F. Wacht, 1971, "A More Constructive Role for Deposit Insurance," *Journal of Finance,* 26 (May), 605-14.

Lindbeck, Assar, 1959, *The "New" Theory of Credit Control in the United States,* (Almqvist and Wiksell, Stockholm).

Lloyd-Davies, Peter R., 1975, "Optimal Financial Policy in Imperfect Markets," *Journal of Financial and Quantitative Analysis,* 10 (September), 457-81.

Long, John B., 1974, "On the Pricing of Corporate Debt: The Risk Structure of Interest Rates, Discussion," *Journal of Finance,* 29 (May), 485-88.

Luckett, Dudley G., 1970, "Credit Standards and Tight Money," *Journal of Money, Credit and Banking,* 2 (November), 420-34.

Mandelker, Gershon, 1974, "Risk and Return: The Case of Merging Firms," *Journal of Financial Economics,* 1 (December), 303-35.

Mayer, Thomas, 1965, "A Graduated Deposit Insurance Plan," *Review of Economics and Statistics,* 47 (February), 114-16.

Mayne, Lucille S., 1972, "Supervisory Influence on Bank Capital," *Journal of Finance,* 27 (June), 637-51.

_____, 1978, "New Directions in Bank Holding Company Supervision," *Banking Law Journal,* 95 (August), 729-42.

Meltzer, Allan H., 1967, "Major Issues in the Regulation of Financial Institutions," *Journal of Political Economy,* 75 (July/August), 482-501.

Merton, Robert C., 1977, "An Analytic Derivation of the Cost of Deposit Insurance and Loan Guarantees," *Journal of Banking and Finance,* 1 (June), 3-11.

_____, 1978, "On the Cost of Deposit Insurance When There Are Surveillance Costs," *Journal of Business,* 51 (July), 439-52.

Meyer, Paul A., and Howard W. Pifer, 1970, "Prediction of Bank Failures," *Journal of Finance,* 35 (September), 853-68.

Michaelsen, Jacob B., and Robert C. Goshay, 1967, "Portfolio Selection and Financial Intermediaries—A New Approach," *Journal of Financial and Quantitative Analysis,* 2 (June), 166-99.

Miller, Merton H., 1977, "Debt and Taxes," *Journal of Finance,* 32 (May), 261-74.

Mingo, John J., 1975, "Regulatory Influence on Bank Capital Investment," *Journal of Finance,* 30 (September), 1111-22.

Moyer, Charles R., and Edward Sussana, 1973, "Registered Bank Holding Company Acquisitions: A Cross-Section Analysis," *Journal of Financial and Quantitative Analysis,* 8 (September), 647-61.

Myers, Stewart C., 1977, "Determinants of Corporate Borrowing," *Journal of Financial Economics,* 5 (July), 147-75.

Orgler, Yair E., 1968, "Selection of Bank Loans for Examination," Unpublished Research Report, Research Division, Federal Deposit Insurance Corporation, (February).

_____, and Benjamin Wolkowitz, 1976, *Bank Capital* (Van Nostrand Reinhold Company, New York).

Orr, Daniel and W. G. Mellon, 1961, "Stochastic Reserve Losses and Expansion of Bank Credit," *American Economic Review,* 51 (September), 614-23.

Peltzman, Sam, 1970, "Capital Investment in Commercial Banking and its Relationship to Portfolio Regulation," *Journal of Political Economy,* 58 (January-February), 1-26.

_____, 1976, "Towards a More General Theory of Regulation," *Journal of Law and Economics,* 19 (August), 211-40.

Pierce, James L., 1966, "Commercial Bank Liquidity," *Federal Reserve Bulletin,* August, 1093-1101.

Porter, Richard C., 1961, "A Model of Bank Portfolio Selection," *Yale Economic Essays,* 1 (Fall), 323-60.

Posner, Richard A., 1974, "Theories of Economic Regulation," *Bell Journal of Economics and Management Science,* 5 (Autumn), 335-58.

Pringle, John J., 1971, "The Role of Capital in the Financial Management of Commercial Banks," Ph.D. dissertation, Stanford University.

_____, 1974, "The Capital Decision in Commercial Banks," *Journal of Finance,* 29 (June), 779-95.

Pyle, David H., 1972, "Descriptive Theories of Financial Institutions Under Uncertainty,"

Journal of Financial and Quantitative Analysis, 7 (December), 2009-29.

Rice, Michael R., 1978, "Financial Impact of Nonbank Activities on Bank Holding Companies," unpublished manuscript; Board of Governors of the Federal Reserve System, (June).

Robinson, Ronald I., and Richard H. Pettway, 1967, *Policies for Optimum Bank Capital,* A study prepared for the Trustees of the Banking Research Fund-Association of Reserve City Bankers.

Ross, Stephen A., 1978, "A Simple Approach to the Valuation of Risky Streams," *Journal of Business,* 51 (July), 453-75.

Rothschild, Michael, and Joseph E. Stiglitz, 1976, "Equilibrium in Competitive Insurance Markets: An Essay on the Economics of Imperfect Information," *Quarterly Journal of Economics,* 90 (November), 629-49.

Roy, Andrew D., 1952, "Safety-First and the Holding of Assets," *Econometrica,* 20 (July), 431- 49.

Sanford, Rose, 1974, "What Really Went Wrong at Franklin National," *Fortune,* (October), 118-21, 220-27.

Santomero, Anthony M., and Ronald D. Watson, 1977, "Determining an Optimal Capital Standard for the Banking Industry," *Journal of Finance,* 32 (September), 1267-82.

_____, and Joseph D. Vinso, 1977, "Estimating the Probability of Failure for Commercial Banks and the Banking System," *Journal of Banking and Finance,* 1 (October), 185-205.

Scott, James H., 1976, "A Theory of Optimal Capital Structure," *Bell Journal of Economics and Management Science,* 7 (Spring), 33-54.

Scott, Kenneth E., and Thomas Mayer, 1971, "Risk and Regulation in Banking: Some Proposals for Federal Deposit Insurance Reform," *Sanford Law Review,* 23 (May), 857-902.

Silverberg, Stanley C., 1975, "Bank Holding Companies and Capital Adequacy," *Journal of Bank Research,* 6 (Autumn), 202-7.

Sinky, Joseph F., 1978, "Identifying 'Problem' Banks, How Do the Banking Authorities Measure A Bank's Risk Exposure?" *Journal of Money, Credit and Banking,* 10 (May), 184-91.

Smith, Clifford W., 1977, "Alternative Methods for Raising Capital: Right Versus Underwitten Offerings," *Journal of Financial Economics,* 5 (December), 273-307.

Spencer, Roger W., 1974, "Channels of Monetary Influence: A Survey," *Federal Reserve Bank of St. Louis Review,* November, 8-26.

Swary, Itzhak, 1977, "Corporate Tax Asymmetry and Optimal Leverage," The Jerusalem School of Business Administration, Working Paper No. 77-04, April.

Taggart, Robert A., and Stuart I. Greenbaum, 1978, "Bank Capital and Public Regulation," *Journal of Money, Credit and Banking,* 10 (May), 158-69.

Talley, Samuel H., 1975, "Bank Holding Companies Financing," *Proceedings of A Conference on Bank Structure and Competition,* Federal Reserve Bank of Chicago, May 1 and 2, 124-35.

Telser, Lester G., 1955-56, "Safety-First and Hedging," *Review of Economic Studies,* 23 (February), 1-16.

United States Congress, 1956, *Bank Holding Company Act of 1956.* (70 Stat. 133), May 9, 1956.

_____, 1970, *Bank Holding Company Act Amendments of 1970,* (Public Law 91-607), December 31, 1970.

Vojta, George J., 1973, *Bank Capital Adequacy,* First National City Bank, New York, February.

Warner, Jerold B., 1977, "Bankruptcy Costs: Some Evidence," *Journal of Finance,* 32 (May), 337-47.

Watson, Ronald D., 1974, "Insuring a Solution to the Bank Capital Hassle," *Business Review,* Federal Reserve Bank of Philadelphia, July-August, 3-18.

Woodworth, Walter G., 1967, "Theories of Cyclical Liquidity Management of Commercial Banks," *National Banking Review,* 4 (June), 377-96.

Wu, Hsiu-Kwang, 1969, "Bank Examiner Criticism, Bank Loan Defaults, and Bank Loan Quality," *Journal of Finance,* 26 (June), 695-705.

Index

Activity constraints
   definition of, 40, 45
   in the decision-making process of
      individual banks, 49, 50, 53-54
   See also Portfolio constraints
Akerlof, George A., on credit market
   equilibrium in underdeveloped
   countries, 135-36
Altman, Edward I., on predicting corporate
   failure, 59
American Bankers Association, on capital
   adequacy requirements, 1
Asia, capital adequacy requirements in, 42

Bank examination, purposes of, 42, 49, 51-52
Bank failure
   before 1971, 42, 59, 138
   definition of, 1
   factors affecting the probability of,
      15, 26, 42, 48, 54, 138
   mortgage subsidiaries as a cause of,
      in BHCs, 105
   risk of, within BHCs, 66-68, 74
   See also Bankruptcy; Problem banks;
      Safety-first constraint
Bank holding companies
   background on, 61-64
   definitions of, 61
   investment incentive in, 68-69
   proposed regulations for, 67-69
   synergistic merger of subsidiaries with,
      64, 73
   See also Nonbank expansion, BHC
Bank Holding Company Act
   1970 Amendment to, 62, 65, 69, 73, 140
   present administration of, 70
   provisions of, 61, 75, 77, 106-7
Banking Act of 1933, on interest rates for
   deposits, 22
Bank of America, application for nonbank
   expansion of, 69-70, 75
Bank regulation
   costs of, 55-58
   effect of, on bank-customer relations, 46, 53
   proposed improvements in, 6-7, 57-60

rationales for, 37-38
   social costs and benefits of, 4-6, 52-57
   use of bank examination in, 42
   use of deposit insurance in, 42-43
   use of portfolio constraints in, 38-42
   See also Activity constraints; Bank
      holding companies; Capital adequacy
      regulation; Loan size constraints;
      Portfolio constraints; Reserve
      requirements
Bank regulators
   as an interest group, 2, 56, 77, 107, 115
   measuring the performance of, 140
   on risk-related insurance rates, 59
Bankruptcy
   costs of, 11-12
   possibility of, as a factor in credit
      portfolio selection, 16-17, 30
   possibility of, as a rationale for bank
      regulation, 37
   relation of collateral to the costs of, 20
   See also Bank failure; Safety-first
      constraint
Banks, unregulated
   bundling charges for products of, 21-23
   credit portfolio selection in, 15-21
   customer-bank relations in, 21
   definition of, 135
   financing decisions of, 21-26, 31
   framework for analyzing decision-making
      processes in, 9-12, 119-22
   information costs in, 13-14
   investment decisions of, 13-21, 30-33
   liquidity management of, 25-26
   loan agreements in, 13
   model of financing decisions in, 26-30
   theory of decision-making
      processes in, 30-36
Barnett, Robert E., on bank failure, 56, 59
Baxter, Nevins D., on bankruptcy costs, 11
Beaver, William H., on predicting corporate
   failure, 59
Belgium, portfolio constraints in, 40-41
Benston, George J.
   on bank behavior, 9, 11, 23

on bank failure, 5, 42, 135
on bank regulation, 37-38, 51, 55, 141
Beverly Hills Bancorp, the failure of, 66, 141
Black, Fischer
    on BHCs, 66, 68, 70
    on bank regulation, 37-38, 56-57
    on customer-bank relations, 14, 21
Blair, Roger D., on the consequences
    of capital adequacy regulation, 5
Burns, Arthur, on the public interest motive
    of bank regulation, 56

Canada, deposit insurance in, 139
Capital adequacy
    definition of, 135
    previous research on, 3
    vs. optimal capital, 3
Capital adequacy regulation
    alternative approaches to, 6-7
    American Bankers Association on, 1
    bank examination as a means of, 42
    decision-making processes in
        banks under, 43-52
    deposit insurance as a means of, 42-43
    effect of, on bank's market value, 52-54
    impact of, on bank's capital, 3-4
    in relation to BHCs, 75-76, 116
    objectives of this study of, 1, 7-8, 111
    portfolio constraints as a type of, 38-42
    previous research on, 3-7
    social costs and benefits of, 4-6, 52-57
    summary of this study of, 111-16
Capital market, data from
    suggested use of, to assess banks' overall
        risk-variance, 58-59, 116
    use of, in this study of nonbank
        expansion by BHCs, 80-84
Citcorp, application for nonbank
    expansion of, 69
Cohen, Kalman J., on the Federal Reserve
    capital adequacy formula, 6
Cotter, Richard V., on the identification of
    problem banks, 5-6
Credit portfolio selection
    by unregulated banks, 15-21, 117-18
    collateral considerations in, 20, 137
    effect of regulations on, 48
    evaluation of, by bank examination, 51
    in relation to risk-related insurance rates, 59
    optimal amount granted to each
        borrower in, 31
    role of bank-customer relations in, 21
    See also Banks, unregulated

Decision-making processes. See Banks,
    unregulated
Deposit insurance

effect of, on capital adequacy, 4, 6
individual bank's decision-making
    process under, 49-50
in the U.S., 42
proposed risk-related premiums for, 59-60
purposes of, 43, 139
See also Capital adequacy regulation
Deposits
    as liabilities of commercial banks, 9-10
    bundling pricing systems for, 22-23
    structure of the market for, 21-24, 137
    tax considerations in, 23, 138
    unexpected withdrawals from, 26
"Direct" chance constraint
    as a basis for evaluating the effectiveness
        of regulation, 44-45
    effect of, on a bank's assets and
        liabilities, 123-25
Diversification of assets. See loan
    size constraints

England. See United Kingdom
Equity capital
    as a liability of commercial banks, 10
    constraints on, 40,45
    structure of the market for, 24
    See also Banks, unregulated; Capital
        adequacy regulations

Federal Deposit Insurance Corporation
    function of, 2, 139
    on problem banks and bank failure, 5-6,
        43, 56
    protection of, by bank regulation, 38, 50-52
Federal Reserve Board
    Bank Holding Company Act mandate to,
        61-62
    "go-slow" policy of, 64, 69-70, 107-9
    on capital adequacy, 2, 6-7
    on government bonds, 25
    on nonbank expansion by BHCs, 62-64,
        75-77, 106-7
    on the regulation of BHCs, 67, 73
Financing decisions
    of BHCs, 65
    of regulated banks, 53
    of unregulated banks, 21-26, 31
First Chicago, application for nonbank
    expansion of, 69
Foreign exchange operations, 41, 140
Franklin National Bank, failure of,
    59, 139, 141

Germany
    bundling pricing systems for deposits in, 23
    portfolio constraints in, 37, 41
Greenbaum, Stuart I., on capital adequacy, 3

Heggestad, Arnold A.
  on BHCs, 65-66
  on capital adequacy regulation, 5, 54
Hodgman, Donald R., on customer-bank
  relations, 21
Holland, Robert C., on the nonbank
  expansion of BHCs, 141-42
Holland. *See* Netherlands
Horvitz, Paul M., on bank failure, 56, 59, 139

India, deposit insurance in, 139
Information
  acquisition and analysis of, by commercial
    banks, 13-14
  as a factor in banks' decision-making
    processes, 9
  costs of, defined, 136
  effects of bank regulation on, 53-54
  effects of nonbank expansion by BHCs
    on, 65
  function of, in credit portfolio selection, 15
  relation of collateral to, 20
Investment decisions
  of BHCs, 65, 68-69
  of regulated banks, 38-42, 53-54
  of unregulated banks, 13-21, 30-33
Ireland, constraints on banking practices in,
  40, 138
Israel
  bundling pricing systems for deposits
    in, 23
  constraints on foreign exchange
    operations in, 41

Jessee, Michael A., on risk in BHCs, 70-71

Kahane, Yehuda, on the consequences of
  capital adequacy regulation, 5
Kaufman, George G., on the failure of the
  Franklin National Bank, 139
Kraus, Alan, on bankruptcy costs, 11
Kreps, Clifton H., on deposit insurance
  and capital adequacy regulation,
  6, 50, 139

Lebanon, deposit insurance in, 139
Leverage constraint
  effect of, on individual banks' decision-
    making processes, 50, 53
  See also Capital adequacy regulation;
    Equity capital
Liquidity management
  by unregulated banks, 25-26
  constraints on, 40-41, 45
Litzenberger, Robert H., on bankruptcy
  costs, 11

Lloyd-Davies, Peter R., on bankruptcy
  costs, 11
Loan agreements
  as compensation for the quality of
    the loan, 136
  characteristics of, 13
  in the private lending market, 57
Loans. *See* Credit portfolio selection
Loan size constraints
  as a type of portfolio constraint, 39-40, 49
  in the decision-making process of
    individual banks, 45, 50, 53
Loans to interested parties, 39-40
Luckett, Dudley G., on customer-bank
  relations, 21
Luxemburg, loan size constraint in, 39

Mayne, Lucille S.
  on BHCs, 66, 70
  on the effectiveness of capital adequacy
    regulation, 3-4
Merton, Robert C., on deposit insurance, 139
Meyer, Paul A., on improving the regulatory
  process, 6-7
Miller, Merton H.
  on BHCs, 66, 68, 70
  on bank regulation, 37-38, 56-57
Mingo, John J.
  on deposit insurance, 52
  on the effectiveness of capital
    adequacy regulation, 4
  on the leverage position of BHCs, 65
Money market funds
  commercial banks as borrowers of, 10,
    24-26, 137
  relation of certificates of deposit, capital
    notes, Eurodollars, federal funds, and
    Federal Reserve loans to, 24
Mortgage companies, affiliated
  BHCs' acquisition of, 74,76
  effect of BHCs' applications to acquire,
    84, 90-92, 94-96, 102-5
  See also Nonbank expansion, BHC
Mortgage companies, independent, 102-6,
  129-34, 143

National Bank of San Diego, the failure of,
  141
Netherlands, portfolio constraint in,
  40-41
Nonbank expansion, BHC
  alternate hypotheses of, 73-75, 102-3
  alternate hypotheses of the Board's denial
    orders on, 75-77, 103-4
  cost-benefit considerations of, 69-71
  de novo activity in, 74, 106-7, 143

development of, 62-64
effect on returns to stockholders of
    applications for, 80-96, 127-28
empirical results of this study of, 84-102
evaluation of current regulations
    concerning, 105-9
financing rationale for, 65
interpretation of this study of, 102-5
investment rationale for, 65
methodology, sample, and data sources
    for this study of, 77-84, 142
shift in risk caused by applications for,
    83-84, 97-102, 107-9
Nonmortgage companies, effect of BHCs'
    applications to acquire, 86-89, 93, 95-96

Orgler, Yair E.
    on bank examination, 51
    on BHCs, 66, 70

Peltzman, Sam
    on deposit insurance, 52
    on the effectiveness of capital adequacy
        regulation, 4
Pettway, Richard H., on capital adequacy, 3
Pifer, Howard W., on improving the
    regulatory process, 6-7
Portfolio constraints
    as a means of protecting the FDIC, 50-51
    as a type of bank regulation, 38
    financing decisions under, 38-39
    individual bank's decision-making process
        under, 45-51
    in relation to bank failure, 42
    investment decisions under, 39-40
    suggested elimination of, 57-58
Posner, Richard A.
    on BHCs, 66, 68, 70
    on bank regulation, 37-38, 56-57
Pringle, John J.
    on capital adequacy, 3
    on the loan market in relation to banks, 136
Problem banks, the identification of, 5-7

Regulation, bank. See Bank regulation
Reserve requirements
    in the decision-making process of
        individual banks, 45
    in relation to liquidity management
        constraints, 40-41, 138
Rice, Michael R., on nonbank expansion by
    BHCs, 84, 105
Robinson, Ronald I., on capital adequacy, 3

Safety-first constraint
    effect of collateral on, 20-21
    explanation of, 16-17
    in the decision-making process of
        regulated banks, 48
    in relation to the direct chance constraint, 44
Santomero, Anthony M.
    on identifying problem banks, 6-7, 57, 108
    on the social costs and benefits of increased
        capitalization, 4-5
Scott, James H., on bankruptcy costs, 11
Silverberg, Stanley C.
    on bank failure, 56, 59
    on BHCs, 66, 70
Sinky, Joseph F., on the identification of
    problem banks, 5-6, 51
Smith, Clifford W., Jr.
    on bank behavior, 9,11
    on interest for deposits, 23
    on transaction costs of raising additional
        equity capital, 24
South America, capital adequacy
    requirements in, 42
Southern California Bank, the failure of, 66
Stock prices. See Capital market, data from
Switzerland, portfolio constraints in, 41

Taggart, Robert A., on capital adequacy, 3

United Kingdom
    countries that follow the tradition of
        bank supervision in, 41
    portfolio constraints in, 39-41
    proposed deposit insurance in, 139
Unregulated banks. See Banks, unregulated

Vinso, Joseph D., on identifying problem
    banks, 6-7, 57, 108
Vojta, George J., on capital requirements
    of regulatory agencies, 2, 7

Wacht, Richard F., on deposit insurance
    and capital adequacy regulation,
    6, 50, 139
Warner, Jerold B., on bankruptcy costs, 11
Watson, Ronald D., on social costs and
    benefits of increased capitalization, 4-5
Western Europe, capital adequacy
    requirements in, 42
Wolkowitz, Benjamin, on BHCs, 66, 70
Wu, Hsiu-Kwang, on bank examination, 51